The Importance of Embracing Jesus

A Guided Journey through the Gospels

Glenn Strauss, M.D.

The Importance of Embracing Jesus

© Copyright 2024 Glenn Strauss, M.D.
ISBN: 978-1-962848-06-0

All Scripture quotations are from the King James Version of the Bible and are public domain.

Interior graphics and cover design: Marji Laine
Editing: Karen Steinmann

Published by:
Roaring Lambs Publishing
17110 Dallas Parkway, Suite 260
Dallas, TX 75248

Published in the United States of America.

Contents

Dedication

This book is dedicated to my grandkids, who I hope will embrace Jesus and stand strong in their faith.

Grandma and I want you to know that we have done our best to be shoulders to stand on so that you can see much further down the path to His Kingdom than we ever could.

With all my love to each of you,
Pop

Introduction

My journey as an author began as an epiphany. I realized that as a follower of Jesus, I was not just learning about God; I was also learning about being human! Not only was Jesus calling me to know His Father; He was also calling me to know *myself* as a human being created in the image of His Father. After all, He claimed to be both the Son of God and the Son of Man. When Jesus invited a seemingly random group of misfits to follow Him, He was opening the door for them to see what it meant to be children of God, made in His image. For me, it was a huge and largely unexplored shift in thinking.

It led to the writing of my first book, *Finding the Way* (Amazon Books, 2019), in which I briefly explore the many times the Creator lovingly pulls humanity back from the brink of disaster while trying to reconnect us with the purpose of our wonderfully complex divine design. But this led me to consider how our design actually works. What specifically about our divine design is so important to the Creator's plan? And if we are that important, and somehow even necessary for God's plan, how did we end up in such a mess?

These questions resulted in the writing of *The Importance of Being Human* (Roaring Lambs Publishing, 2023). In this second book, I delve into what it means to be made in the image of God, and I expose the enormous challenges we face today in a world filled with myths about creation and human identity. The book explores the crucial questions we must address if we are to recover what it means to be human in a culture bent on denying us our value and true self. It offers a reminder that humanity was designed to create love and meaning in our world. My conclusion is that the final solution to the chaos of our world is to fully immerse ourselves in the life of Jesus, our Designer and Sustainer. To restore any hope for humanity, we must embrace Jesus. But *how* then, practically speaking, do we do so? The answer to that question lies in this book.

About this Book

The Importance of Embracing Jesus is the final installment in the series written to undo the thinking that traps so many of us in spiritually dead-end lives. If we are to reverse the trends of destructive cultural patterns and an impotent Church, we must go beyond seeing Jesus as merely the Way to heaven and the Truth we need to dogmatize. We must see Him as the Giver of Life—the One source reinvigorating us and our damaged world. It is imperative that we embrace Jesus as the ever present, always good, forever loving Creator bent on restoring His creation to its full potential!

I love how John the Apostle says it some years after His time with Jesus on earth:

> *"We know that the Royal Son of God has been here on earth and has given us all we need to know the truth. I am confident of this because we, His followers, immersed ourselves in the One who we discovered is the Truth—Jesus, the Messianic representative of God. He is fully God and He Himself is the eternal Life we hoped for"*
> *(1 John 5:20, my paraphrase).*

In John's eyes, Jesus was, in fact, the Way, the Truth, *and* the Life (John 14:5-6).

This book will help you see through the eyes of Jesus' biographers (primarily Matthew and John) as they describe their real-life experiences with Him. They discovered that their time with Jesus was not just exposure to a new way of life; it was an encounter with eternal Life itself, not a new philosophy or a new political movement, and certainly not a religious experience! I am inviting you to sit at the feet of the Gospel writers as they offer us a look at what their experience was like.

This book is a guide for the journey—offering you a road map through their writings. As an added feature, it provides tools that, when used on your journey, become a powerful mechanism for change. The tools in this study tap into all components of our design—body, mind, and spirit. This book is not designed for a certain type of personality or specific style of learning. As a cross-cultural trainer and educator for many years, I've learned that substantial growth as an individual requires intentional engagement of all the aspects of our divine design as human beings, regardless of our personalities. The path to personal growth provided here is not designed for you as an individual but for you as a human being!

I realize that those with no margin left in their lives will be hoping for something quick or efficient. You may be looking for a little help in your spiritual life, not an overhaul! Too often I hear that spiritual life is a series of tedious exercises. We listen to inspiring messages, maybe read a bit in the latest self-help book, try our best to be nice, and go to church as often as we can. I would love to sit down with you over a cup of coffee and discuss how this book offers something different—something more. It taps into your fundamental design as a human being and connects you with a unique framework for personal growth.

The fact is, we should all *expect* to grow—we are alive after all, and living things grow and change. The challenge is choosing the right path. I believe everything you need to establish a transformative rhythm in your life is within reach. But you will need the help of those who knew Jesus the best and a few specific tools to get you going in the right direction. To make the path a little easier to find, I have written myself into the pages as your personal guide. I would be honored for you to give it a try. It only takes a few weeks to discover how much this strategy has to offer!

For those early followers of Jesus, immersing themselves in His life was the privilege of a lifetime. The road ahead was not easy for them, and it will not be easy for us. But embracing Jesus is totally worth it! Together we can take a journey that changes everything.

Before You Begin

Imagine for a moment what it would be like if you could fully immerse yourself in the life and teachings of Jesus—to be one of those early followers, perhaps even one of the disciples chosen to walk with Him the last few years of His life. Okay, I realize when you got out of bed today, you weren't thinking how much fun it might be to wander around in the desert with no toilets or air conditioning, to live off donations and often fear for your life. But you must admit, it would be exciting to follow a man who cast out demons, raised people from the dead, controlled the weather, and confronted the authorities. And while doing all these things, He humbly aligned Himself with the poor and the outcast.

The fact is, Jesus *has* invited us to immerse ourselves in His Life, not in the nitty gritty of survival in the Ancient Middle East, but in a unique way of doing Life here today. Understanding a life lived 2,000 years ago presents a huge challenge. We only get small glimpses of all that happened in the life of Jesus; we find it difficult to know the exact details. And what we do know is often culturally confusing or lacking in detail. His three years of active ministry are reduced to several thousand words in a foreign language attributed by tradition to four different biographers (Matthew, Mark, Luke, and John) who wrote some twenty to thirty years after Jesus returned to His heavenly realm. How can we possibly immerse ourselves in the Life of Jesus with such limited and often confusing information?

Is It Really Possible?

Have you ever wondered why Jesus didn't write His own book or autobiography? Wouldn't it be nice to have Jesus' ministry notes? It would certainly make it easier for us today. Jesus did a lot of reading and praying in private, but as far as we know, He did not write down a thing. No one has discovered the writings of Jesus recorded on a scroll in some archaeological dig. There is no *Kingdom Life for Dummies,* published *circa C.E. 33.* What's more, He never directed His disciples to go to the synagogue to study like other rabbinic students of His day. Instead, He discussed the issues with His followers as He walked alongside them. He reflected on the Torah, the Psalms, and the Prophets. He prayerfully engaged with His Father away from the pressures of day-to-day interactions and religious activities.

So clear and powerful was this unique rabbinic strategy that Jesus' disciples came to think of Him as "*the* Word." Jesus didn't want His disciples to have their eyes down in their books or on their class notes. He didn't want them to be entangled by meaningless arguments and discussions leading nowhere. He simply wanted them to have their eyes up on Him!

As far as we know, these chosen Apostles went on to spend the rest of their lives immersed in the Life of Jesus, sharing their personal experiences with others, and literally giving up their own lives for Him. With the help and inspiration of the Holy Spirit, a few of them wrote down some of what they lived, believed, and taught. These were not trained historians or theologians. Nor were they experienced authors and poets. They did not even have first-hand knowledge of many of the events they recorded. (For example, none of them were there at the birth of Jesus.) But their writings tell a story of the events and teachings of the Rabbi who deeply affected them—the One they came to know as the Messiah. They were convinced He was the One promised by God as the Rescuer of the whole world, not just their own nation.

No doubt they spent a good bit of time talking amongst themselves about what and who they saw and heard and even physically touched alongside Jesus. (Think for a minute about all the sick people they brought to Him!) It took years of discussion and reflection for the disciples to put together all that had happened. No wonder it took a while before they wrote any of it down! I suspect they even used some trial and error to work out effective ways to explain it so others could see Jesus like they did. As a result, these authors did not write like Sunday school teachers; they wrote as people immersed in a way of life they wanted to share with others.

The Apostle John beautifully summarizes their experiences:

"What was from the beginning of time, but we today have heard and seen and touched with our own hands, *regarding Life itself,* this we proclaim so that all may share the experience of Life as we did, fully immersed in the Life of Jesus" (1 John 1: 1-5, my paraphrase).

Clearly, the disciples believed that Jesus made the fullness of Life real and available to all.

This leads to an important question: Is it really possible today for *me* to immerse myself in the Life of Jesus, and if so, how? For many years, I thought the answer involved getting all the facts right through careful study and analysis, proper contextualization, even learning the original language. This approach was satisfying and productive on many levels but never truly immersive. It turns out the answer was right in front of me in the writings of Jesus' biographers. They were inviting me to immerse myself in His life, not analyze it. I needed to learn to think like a Gospel writer.

Is It New Or Just Different?

The Importance of Embracing Jesus is the direct result of my efforts to think like those who first taught the way of Jesus. It will introduce you to a new strategy for learning and, in the process, will also give you a new perspective on the Gospels. As you go from week to week, you will see that the Gospel writers do not simply tell stories or record teachings anecdotally. They invite you to get caught up with them in their discussions and the challenges they experienced. The Apostles draw you into a dialogue with Jesus that displays their unbelief and lack of understanding as well as the loving nature of the One they were following. Their writing leads us all to see the questions *they* should have been asking so *we* can get it right. "Who's the greatest?" should have been "Who's the least?" "How do we get the children out of the way?" should have been "How do we become more like children ourselves?" The Gospel writers give us a great start in discovering how to ask questions that can make us all into lifelong learners in the ways of Jesus.

You may want to note here that most of the other New Testament documents are personal letters written to address specific issues. Only the four Gospels and Acts are written to help us see the significance of the events that unfolded during and shortly after the life of Jesus on earth. The authors of the personal epistles (primarily Paul) use analytical and often harsh language to address specific problems. The Gospel writers, on the other hand, use stories and experiences to teach and immerse the audience in the life of Jesus and His early followers. To be sure, a story lies behind each Apostolic letter, but the language is not story-telling language. The Gospel writers use historical narrative to weave together what they each considered key events, and they do so in a way that exposes a bigger story and a deeper meaning. This is why the Gospel writers never give us bullet point spirituality or four steps to eternal life. The "gospel" message is the story they tell.

To be clear, the details of every story and every teaching written by Jesus' biographers are important. It is the written, inspired Word of God. From one point of view, I am not offering anything new here. But from another, what you will explore is quite different because the perspective or framework for looking at the facts is different. For example, I personally love the story of Lazarus being called out of his tomb by a tearful Jesus. The words of the story are dramatic and powerful (John 11:1–12:17). The facts are clear. But to immerse myself in the story of Lazarus requires asking why John tells this specific story in this specific way at this point in his writing. Jesus has raised others from the dead—so what is different about this story? Why for these particular people at this particular time? Why do we see Lazarus walking out of an open tomb still bound in grave clothes instead of finding him as he sits up and takes his first breath? And how might this story relate to the story Jesus tells earlier of the rich man asking Abraham to send Lazarus to come and comfort him (Luke 16:19-31)? How might this all relate to Jesus' resurrection? What's the bigger story here that John is telling?

Discussing these questions with others led me to realize that the story of Lazarus is the turning point in a larger narrative John is communicating. Jesus is risking His life for a friend to lead him out of a grave back to life. But this would not be the final resurrection for Lazarus. Here, Jesus sets in motion the final events that ensured His own death on the cross and a final resurrection for Himself and all who followed Him. Jesus is demonstrating what love looks like with foreshadowing of what His own victorious resurrection will look like. No wonder He sheds empathetic tears. I could say more, but I hope you can hear that I learned a lot from these discussions!

Sometimes, answers about Jesus don't come from studying the details—the most important questions are not answered by more analysis of isolated facts about Him. Instead, solutions to our questions require imagination and conversations with others who believe in Him. It turns out that discussions with those who are "new creations" in Christ (2 Corinthians 5:17) will provide fresh perspectives on the Life He offers! Immersing ourselves in the life of Jesus requires engagement with other people who have the mind of Christ (1 Corinthians 2:16). You can come up with some good ideas on your own, but sometimes the best way for Jesus to get our attention is in our conversations, not in our churches! I would strongly recommend that you review Appendix 1 for more information on how to start conversations that can grow into a personal community of faith.

But there is another critical issue to consider: Once you start seeing the reality of Life in Jesus, you will need to develop some disciplines to help you integrate what you discover into your own life. You can't sit around discussing all day. So, what can you do to carry it with you and make it part of your daily life? This is why each topic includes instructions to write down a few thoughts, take time to read the brief devotional for reflection, and spend a little time with God, quieting yourself to give your spirit (not your mind) a chance to hear His Voice. These components engage specific learning components of your brain and your spirit. (For the learning geeks among us, check out authors such as John Dowling, Andrew Newberg, and Timothy Jennings to dig deeper into the science of it.) Intellectual stimulation is not enough. Expectation and good intentions are not enough. Reflection and time alone with God are both needed to build your capacity for spiritual Life. When you finish reading this chapter, please take a few minutes to look at Appendix 2. It provides useful tips on how to spend time with God.

All this to say that it's great to begin with discussion, but that's not all there is to it. Discussion will shed new light on what you know. But it doesn't matter how much Light there is if your soul can't receive it. Your soul needs a few disciplines like writing, reflection, and quietness before the Lord to really flourish. A healthy soul is able to receive Light. What's truly exciting is that this Light is then reflected in the choices you make!

How Does It Work?

The Importance of Embracing Jesus is built on a holistic learning paradigm. I used this as a model successfully for many years in cross-cultural surgical and spiritual skills training. In this approach, I did not tell students what they needed to know. I *walked with them* through an immersive learning process. I acted as a guide to help them explore their aptitudes as well as the knowledge and skills they would need for success. Trainees would learn a bit, do a bit, ask lots of questions, take in more information, adapt, do more, and enjoy the reward of a more satisfying experience. I am happy to say that in many cases, this ended up with ophthalmic trainees becoming highly proficient surgeons. But equally exciting is that pastors hired to be translators and several technicians on our ophthalmic team grew into church planters and disciple makers while practicing a trade they could use to support themselves and their families.

This model worked because participants were motivated by the joy of discovery, a respectful learning environment, and experiences that inspired them. My best students were *not* necessarily the smartest or those who learned the fastest or those who only did what I said to do. The most successful were those who knew how to ask the right questions and who were excited to explore their skills and ideas with others! (You can learn more about this teaching model in Jane Vella's book, *Training Through Dialogue: Promoting Effective Learning and Change with Adults.*[1])

Don't misunderstand: I think you will find that *The Importance of Embracing Jesus* is more than just a good training system for deep learning. It's designed to help you explore the Life and teachings of Jesus as a journey of personal transformation. It's constructed to help you go beyond gathering information to immersive discovery and internalization. It moves you along a path towards the love and meaning you are designed to create during your lifetime (read more about this in *The Importance of Being Human)*. It works by creating the expectation that everyone, including you, has a critical part to play

---

[1] Jane Vella, *Training Through Dialogue: Promoting Effective Learning and Change with Adults,* Jossey-Bass, 1995.

in life! In my experience, the biggest barrier to personal growth is not lack of intelligence or lack of good intentions. The biggest barrier is failure to realize that you as a follower of Jesus have something to offer someone else on the same journey because you are a new creation with the mind of Christ. Most people find this very hard to believe.

The model I propose here is not new, but it has been largely forgotten. Early Church fathers promoted the simple disciplines of study, meditation, contemplation, and service. They viewed these practices as the essence of Christian life. Today, the original practices of Christianity have been largely replaced by the business practices of Christianity. Sadly, our churches tend to be more about the numbers, business models, and infotainment. It's no wonder, since the massive infrastructure of many churches is a financially hungry beast to feed. Church leaders rely on models designed to efficiently reach the most people and bring them into the church. I know it's usually well-intentioned. But I have to ask, who or what's driving Christianity today? If we have gotten more efficient with spreading the message, why are conditions getting worse in our world? Why do our biggest churches seem more like marketing campaigns than transformational communities? Why is Bible illiteracy growing, not shrinking?

Perhaps it's time to reimagine how we do church based on what Jesus did, rather than what we have done for the past 100 years or so. Maybe we should ask ourselves how *Kingdom* growth works and how it contrasts with *church* growth models. Let me summarize two big ideas for consideration.

First, what if we could build a culture within Christianity based on the expectation that all people are truly created in the image of God? Rather than starting with the assumption that everyone needs to be saved (though this is true), we start with the conviction that there is something about our God-given design worth saving. What if we learned to value the enhancements God has given every believer that make Jesus visible in our badly damaged world (see Part 3 of *The Importance of Being Human*)? In short, what if we begin by recognizing the importance of being human?

Secondly, what if we gathered with followers of Jesus expecting that, as newly created beings, we are capable of acting like members of a new spiritual Kingdom? Rather than starting with the assumption that we need someone to tell us what to believe and convince us to do the right thing (encouragement we often really do need!), we start with the conviction that as His followers, we can actually embrace Jesus Himself and bring something of Him to others, no matter how much we know about Christianity or how messy our lives are. What if we retool churches to reveal God at work rather than man at work? What if we begin by recognizing the importance of embracing Jesus first and foremost?

Again, please do not misunderstand my intention here. *The Importance of Embracing Jesus* is not about getting rid of churches; it's about encouraging a new kind of culture within Christianity that generates expectant and healthy discussions in our churches or wherever followers of Jesus meet. Meeting together in large groups for worship is still critical to remind us of the scale of the work God is doing, but it is not the main platform for transformation. Even fellowship groups are usually too big, though this is a step in the right direction. We need to retool churches and growth groups so that they, more often than not, produce genuine growth.

It's not that complicated: It requires small groups of four or five discussing ideas just like you might do with any group of friends. No specific leader is required—just something to give it spiritual direction and a mutual expectation that God is at work. This type of culture can develop anywhere, anytime, with any group. I truly hope it does so within our churches, but we dare not forget that Jesus can and does show up in any social context. I pray this book stirs something in you and becomes one of the tools for the development of a culture of transformation. I hope this book contributes to healthy discussion among your friends and church leaders today about what it means to truly embrace Jesus.

Is This A Bible Study?

In case you haven't noticed, I have avoided referring to this guide as a "Bible study." The phrase causes all sorts of reactions without giving much clarity. *The Importance of Embracing Jesus* is a guide that uses the Bible as a means to an end, not as an end in itself. It will help you connect the stories and the teachings of Jesus with a bigger Story—hopefully weaving them into a beautiful tapestry that enriches and expands your mind and heart. This guide provides a framework that encourages you to use reading, group discussion, journaling, devotional reflection, and time alone with God as tools for change. But the group you meet with is the real resource! You will learn more about each of these tools as you work your way through the book.

The topic for each week is presented as a series of four carefully constructed questions that will help you immerse yourself in discussion about the life of Jesus. Think of it as a means to engage in a story, rather than doing a study. My goal is to encourage you to engage in a dialogue that takes you beyond Bible study to the big picture surrounding the stories of the early followers of Jesus. There is meaning in the stories that can only be seen with the help of others. It is the dialogue that makes this more of what I would call a "Jesus study" rather than a Bible study!

This strategy doesn't change a thing about the beauty of the individual stories. Nor does it change the powerful words spoken by Jesus and written by His followers. Nor is it an attempt to add or take anything away from the Truth. The framework provided here is intended to add layers of meaning to what you learn and know! Discussion, personal reflection, and taking time to quiet your mind for spiritual listening to the Voice of Jesus allows the bigger story to filter into the deepest parts of your being. Used together, the tools found here will help you live in the story of the Gospel writers. It's a story so profound, it started a world-changing cultural movement.

I realize that most of us were raised to value facts, not questions. We trust "truth," not narrative. Stories are presumed to be fiction. Maybe that is why we tend to view the Bible as inspired facts, not stories. We study rather than imagine our way to understanding. We are comfortable sitting in classrooms and in churches just listening to someone else think. We enjoy reducing Truth to a few bullet points, one-liners, bumper stickers, refrigerator magnets with Bible verses, and church slogans. But where's the fun in that?

This guide is intended to produce a type of growth you can't get from studying on your own, sitting in a classroom, or attending a church service. It's designed to inspire discussions that spark epiphanies which can be integrated into your life! You will learn to ask questions—good questions—and learn to think more clearly. It will expand your spiritual capacity and your relationships. You will learn the difference between facts and meaning. You will learn to explore with others, and with a little effort, I think you will find that an exciting, awe-inspiring Story begins to unfold, with you right in the middle of it! Most importantly, you will find yourself embracing Jesus as He enters the Story with you. Let the fun begin!

How To Use This Discussion Guide

You may have noticed the Table of Contents looks a bit odd. I have set up *The Importance of Embracing Jesus* to engage you as if you are part of a team of investigative reporters. Your job is to immerse yourself in a discussion of the events so that you can get the scoop and find the real story. The Table of Contents lists five feature stories you will develop, along with specific "assignments" (listed as headlines) to explore each week. As your "editor," my role is to suggest lines of questioning and help you put the stories together. I have sequenced the topics like a breaking news story in which you are to be embedded with your team. As one of the reporters, your assignment is to find sources, ask questions, and pursue leads that contribute to the story.

The primary source for your investigation will be the testimony of two eyewitnesses, Matthew and John. To study their testimony, you will need a Bible or Bible app. (Personally, I prefer a hard copy.) Most any translation will do, as long as it's comfortable for reading. However, I would suggest one of the newer readable translations like the English Standard Version, New Living Bible, The Message, or The Passion Translation. It is certainly acceptable to use any Bible with which you are already familiar, but it can be helpful to try a new version just to get a new perspective. Resources like www.bibleproject.com provide an engaging medium to help you explore the back stories of the eyewitnesses and their culture.

For each headline, I will direct you to specific Bible references like "witness testimony" to introduce you to the facts of the case. But the real investigation begins, as I have said, with a second and equally important resource: the discussion with your co-investigators.

To use this book, begin by building or joining a small discussion group. Introduce the idea by asking one simple question: "Are you interested in getting together to discuss some questions I have about Jesus? I think your perspective could be really helpful." Be sure to clarify that it's not a typical Bible study, not a church meeting, and not a way to solicit anything other than thoughtful engagement. A group of four to five people is ideal. Ask those who sit around you in church, those in your home fellowship group, or those you run into regularly in your neighborhood; or consider a regular get-together at the dinner table with family or a weekly get-together with a friend or two over coffee.

Next, use this study guide to organize what you will do as a group. Each chapter has all you need to explore each topic, using four specific questions to prompt a good discussion. It works best if everyone has a copy of this guide, but it's also okay for one person to use the book as a leader's guide. Someone needs to get the group started, but after that, everyone can just follow along using this book as a guide. A separate "leaders guide" is not necessary.

The study is broken into three segments to accommodate a typical spring, summer, and fall meeting schedule. Part 1 consists of Feature Story #1 (eight weeks). It provides the introduction and the framework of events around which Jesus built His entire mission. Part 2 consists of Feature Stories #2 and #3 (eleven weeks). These work nicely together to explain the new spiritual domain introduced by Jesus. Part 3 consists of Feature Stories #4 and #5 (eleven weeks). These stories provide an up-close examination of the nature and character of Jesus as the main character of the bigger Story. Note that Part 1 is a little shorter and can serve as a good starter to try it out. Breaking the study up into segments is not at all necessary, but I recognize the value of occasional breaks.

For optimal use of this material, I would recommend you follow a few basic rules. First, stick to the weekly outline and meet regularly. The material and learning tools are sequenced to create a flow, which is lost if you do it out of order or only meet sporadically. Your personal study time can be adjusted to fit your changing time pressures and your other interests but should take no more than 10 minutes unless you dig in deeper. Time for reflection typically should be about 10 minutes per week, and you should set aside an additional 15 minutes per week for resting quietly in the presence of Jesus. The bulk of your time will be spent discussing the stories. Plan on meeting for at least one hour. If possible, an hour-and-a-half is better. When you add it all up, the total time per week is only about two to two-and-a-half hours.

Second, as you read the references I provide, make it a habit to keep asking, "What's the real story here?" or "What would I do if I was seeing or hearing this for the first time?" Think of yourself as an investigative reporter. Look for what the stories *mean*, not just what the Bible says. If you let it, the Bible will stimulate new thoughts and ideas. Use your discussions to explore ideas, not just to answer the questions I provide. Don't worry if you feel a little unsure about specific facts. Don't worry if you do not always come to a clear conclusion. Don't linger on questions that don't seem to get any discussion going. The purpose is to stimulate critical thinking pathways as you listen for what God is saying through others. Use uncertainty as an opportunity to gather perspectives from everyone in the group and dig deeper. You really do need to hear what everyone has to say.

Finally, this book is designed for you to use as a guide down the path of personal transformation. After all, you are exploring stories that will change lives! Each week I begin with my personal reflection on the subject you have investigated. I invite you to use it for your own personal reflection. Even more important, the end of each chapter includes a key reminder— take time to quiet your mind as you create space for listening with your spirit. Prayerfully "listen" to the Voice that often speaks without words. Christian contemplation, as it is sometimes called, is a powerful tool to expand your spiritual capacity. (Review Appendix 2 for more information on how this works.)

By the way, I am well aware that reflection and time with God are easy steps to skip since no one is there to hold you accountable for doing it except you! Let me encourage you to try the whole strategy for at least three weeks. If you are not convinced it makes a difference, then just continue with the weekly discussions and come back to it later. You can even begin just by reading the reflections as a weekly personal devotional if you prefer and then decide if you want to get a group discussion going. Regardless of how you get there, the maximum benefit comes from including everything offered here.

Let the fun begin

Here is where the fun begins. It's time to get started with the discussions. There are no wrong answers because you are working on finding the right questions! The point is to make connections between the stories and teachings that draw you all into the same framework as a group. I am convinced that when you ask questions about Jesus, He shows up to answer them! I believe this is exactly what Jesus meant when He promised His disciples that His Spirit would be their teacher (John 14:26, 16:13).

Your discussions may be a little chaotic at first. Just focus on listening carefully to what others are saying. It is amazing how Jesus uses others to fill in the gaps in our own thinking. Remember, it's not a competition. It's about listening. I remind you again that some additional help on how to ask good questions to build your group is in Appendix 1. I strongly recommend you review this information before you begin.

As you work through this guide with others, you will discover brand-new angles to the stories that make them more exciting and more impactful than what you ever imagined. Truth will take on new meaning! Over time, the "Headlines" you have explored will serve as a series of beacons, charting your own immersive experiences as you walk through the feature stories with Jesus. Your discussions will grow more intentional and satisfying as you explore the stories together, especially if you are taking time for reflection and spiritual listening.

I would suggest you approach *The Importance of Embracing Jesus* almost playfully, like a child discovering some new and vast imagined world. The questions are designed to be a source of discovery—not a test. But please remember I am not suggesting you make up your own truth. I am saying you can start to see the Truth in a much broader framework by learning to ask the right questions in discussion with others. It's here that you begin to see the stories and teachings connected with profound meaning. You *can* immerse yourself in the life of Jesus!

So welcome to the Jesus Study. I hope it will give you hours of enjoyment. What can be more fun than taking some time out of your routine to immerse yourself with others in the radical life and message of Jesus?

Part 1

A Story Unfolds for All Creation to See

Feature Story #1:
A New Beginning for Humanity

A look at the key events in the story of Jesus.

Let's begin our investigation by exploring key events in the life of Jesus. Overall, the Gospel writers tell the story of a heavenly realm freshly and powerfully restored on earth in a completely unexpected way. It is the long-hidden domain of the Creator of the universe revealed in the man, Jesus of Nazareth. Think of it like you are invited along on a journey with Jesus as He ascends to the throne over all creation, revealed in a new spiritual domain right here on earth. You are part of an investigative reporting team observing, listening, and questioning what you see and hear as this story unfolds.

Our first Feature Story will be built around eight key events that occurred during the ministry of Jesus. When woven together, these eight events create a storyboard compressing three years of incredible encounters into a clear storyline. Each event is worth investigating and, at some point, you may want to go back for further study. Your "job" for now is to investigate how each event contributes to your first Feature Story: "A New Beginning for Humanity." Follow the leads suggested for each Headline and stay focused on the main story. I promise you that it will lead to some incredible discoveries.

For background research, you won't find much information about the early years of Jesus' life, but considerable material is available on the cultural, religious, philosophical, and political influences that affected Jesus and His family as well as His friends. Encourage your "co-investigators" to pursue special interests they may have in these subject areas as the investigation progresses. Find an area of interest you have as well and do some digging. The Internet offers a great tool for topical studies. Developing special interests will contribute significantly to your research, but it's not critical for your discussions.

Your main source of information for this feature story are the four biographers, traditionally assumed to be Matthew, Mark, Luke, and John. Two centuries of investigation have revealed no better sources than these. Their biographical writing is carefully constructed to explain and support the work to which they had given their lives: spreading some extremely good news about Jesus. The main events begin when Jesus is about 30 years old. But for our study, we begin at the beginning with what we know about the birth of Jesus.

Week 1 Headline:

A Miraculous Birth Guarantees Restoration of Our Stolen Birthright

I've always loved the creation story. I can imagine the sadness and grief of Adam and Eve walking away from their garden paradise in shame. But God launches a plan to restore His Presence in creation. He pulls back the curtain on history so we can see a new story literally being born. While time holds still, humble shepherds see a heavenly Kingdom unveiled, with angelic beings announcing the birth of a divine baby. Thirty years before Jesus performs any miracles, the miracle of His birth forever restores the connection between a long-hidden heavenly realm and our decaying earthly realm.

It took me a long time to realize that this is the Christmas miracle. This birth story sets the stage for the return of humanity's royal birthright lost in the Garden of Eden. The privilege of dominion over creation and fellowship with the Creator (our birthright) was stolen by Satan with a few lies. The promise to restore the birthright through Abraham was squandered by his grandson Jacob, who—in a series of offenses—stole the birthright from his brother (Genesis 25:29-34), conspired with his mother to deceive his father for the blessing of the birthright (Genesis 27:1-29), and then fought with God for something easier and quicker (Genesis 32:22-30). Our hope for restoration was lost by a nation in exile for most of its existence. But it was renewed on the first Christmas.

All seemed lost, but then Jesus enters the story. He forever ends the reign of the dreadful deceiver (Satan). Through His divine conception and human birth, He sets the stage for peace on earth and good will from the Creator towards man, just like the angels' song proclaims. Our hope to stand by the Creator's side as kings and priests, free from spiritual exile, was restored by the birth of a King of the Jews unlike any other. As a result, a new Israel (all of us who have and will follow Jesus) would be born from remnants of the old.

For you and me, there is more good news. Jesus, the only begotten Son of God, is still human! Now, we have a sinless, flesh and bones brother in Jesus, with whom to partner with in the work of fully restoring the heavenly realm on earth. Satan will never again be able to steal that which God restored through the birth of an innocent, helpless baby.

Before You Meet:

Spend some time familiarizing yourself with the story you will be investigating. Read Matthew 1:1–2:23, Luke 1:26–2:40, and John 1:10-14. Each of the Gospels adds unique details worth noting, but these details are not the immediate concern of this investigation.

To Begin Your Meeting:

Read this week's headline and then Luke 2:1-40 out loud. Invite Jesus to join you to help answer some questions, and thankfully acknowledge that His Spirit is present as your Helper to guide your discussion. I will remind you to do this each week, but please do not let this become some kind of ritual prayer. Remember, it is an actual invitation.

To Begin Your Discussion:

Read the following introduction out loud to the group:

Sometimes, it is difficult to look beneath the surface of a well-established tradition. The Christmas story is perhaps one of the most familiar of all. On the surface, it appears that God shows up in the Ancient Middle East as a baby boy. But what does this narrative tell us about the profound changes taking place in the spiritual domain? The world knows Jesus as a religious icon born in a manger with angels singing in the background. What does this story tell us is really going on?

Discuss the following questions one at a time.

Read each question out loud and listen to what each person is saying. Ask questions to clarify and develop ideas together as a group. Help each other stay on topic with the reminder, "What does this have to do with the question we are discussing?"

1. What is so important about being human that God would choose to forever become one of us? And why as a baby?

2. Why do the angels sing that the birth of Jesus is about "peace on earth and good will towards man?" Do they mean this literally?

3. How does this Christmas story foreshadow the whole story of Jesus becoming King of the new heavenly Kingdom on earth?

4. Is Jesus still human? And if so, how does this story change our story as human beings?

Note some of the ideas that strike you as especially meaningful:

Before you leave, share one or two of these ideas with the group. It is essential that you take a few minutes to do this before you break up the meeting. Consider having someone act as a notetaker for the group to keep a diary of discussion points and highlights. Keeping a journal for yourself is also helpful.

Close with a prayer of thanksgiving and expectation that God will continue to show you more.

Within a day or two of your discussion, take at least one 15-minute time-out to allow Jesus to have easy access to your heart.

Sit comfortably, close your eyes, with no phone, no Bible, and no notepad. This is a time for you to just be in the presence of Jesus. Always begin by inviting the Holy Spirit to speak. Let thoughts go past you as you use this as sacred time with God. This is spiritual listening, and quiet is the sound of Jesus connecting with your soul, not your conscious mind. Remember that your subconscious mind is working, and your spirit is responding whether you are conscious of it or not.

If this is your first time to try listening to a Voice with no words, be patient and cut yourself some slack. If there is a lot of noise in your head, try using a single word or the phrase of a favorite song to reduce the clutter. With time, you may find a "sacred word" that is very personal to you. Don't focus on the word—just use it to call yourself back from the chaos!

Week 2 Headline:

A Weird Messenger Announces that Jesus Is Bringing a New Type Of Kingdom to Earth

This is one of the stories that I always tend to skip over. It's such a strange scene for you and me to understand today. In a puzzling first move, Jesus aligns Himself with an eccentric wilderness preacher. But why? It's easy to forget that His cousin, John the Baptist, also has a miraculous birth story (Luke 1:5-80) and lives under the prophetic mantle that he will "make ready the way of the Lord" (Isaiah 40:3). John announces a coming Kingdom of God that will be built on personal repentance rather than animal sacrifice. Then Jesus shows up to join his ministry by being baptized.

Sometimes I forget that baptism was more than a church ritual in Jesus' day. Through His baptism by John, Jesus effectively joined a mission to restore the world by repentance, and He stepped into His role as a Rabbi with this specific message. He is endorsed symbolically by Elijah (represented by John in the story), by the literal spoken Word of His Father, and by the physical presence of the Holy Spirit coming upon Him as a dove. During the baptismal ceremony, it becomes clear that Jesus is offering something the world has never seen: the Creator of the universe has, in the water of baptism, anointed Jesus His Son to purify and lead a new repentant people into a new Kingdom.

Before You Meet:

Spend some time familiarizing yourself with the story you will be investigating by reading Luke 1:9-25, Luke 3:1-22, Matthew 3:1-17, Mark 1:1-11, John 1:19-34, and Isaiah 40:3. Note the parallel with Elijah in 2 Kings 1:8. An online Bible is a great resource for looking up multiple references.

To Begin Your Meeting:

Read this week's headline and then Mark 1:1-11 out loud. Invite Jesus to join you to help answer some questions, and thankfully acknowledge that His

Spirit is present as your Helper to guide your discussion. Please do not let this become some kind of ritual prayer. Remember, it is an actual invitation.

To Begin Your Discussion:

Read the following introduction out loud to the group:

How did Jesus become an official Jewish Rabbi? He did not formally attend a rabbinic school as far as we know, though He did study the scriptures as a youth. Instead, Jesus chose to align Himself with His eccentric cousin, John the Baptist's school of teaching. His baptism by John was no ordinary baptism. It was attended by the Creator of the universe and by the Holy Spirit! Jesus was declared fit to be divine royalty that all should follow! What in the world is really going on here?

Discuss the Following Questions One at a Time.

Read each question out loud and listen to what each person is saying. Ask questions to clarify and develop ideas together as a group. Help each other stay on topic with the reminder, "What does this have to do with the question we are discussing?"

1. Why does Jesus specifically seek the water baptism of John as His path to the rabbinic priesthood? Someone read Matthew 3:11 to get the discussion going.

2. Who all attends the baptismal ceremony of Jesus, both physically and spiritually?

3. What is the difference between the symbolic water baptism of John and the coming transformative baptism of Jesus by the Holy Spirit?

Someone read Luke 3:3, Genesis 1:1-2, and John 1:31-33 for comparison.

4. How does the story of a simple baptism set the stage for Jesus' role as the Messiah?

Note some of the ideas that strike you as especially meaningful:

Before you leave, share one or two of these ideas with the group. Read back the notes from Week 1 and add highlights from the current discussion. It is essential that you take a few minutes to do this before you break up the meeting. Consider circulating specific notes or a summary using email, a text group, or other social media tools. Use whatever tool you choose to raise additional questions. Don't forget that keeping a journal for yourself is also helpful.

Close with a prayer of thanksgiving and expectation that God will continue to show you more.

Within a day or two of your discussion, take at least one 15-minute time-out to allow Jesus to have easy access to your heart.

Sit comfortably, close your eyes, with no phone, no Bible, and no notepad. This is a time for you to just be in the presence of Jesus. Always begin by inviting the Holy Spirit to speak. Let thoughts go past you as you use this as sacred time with God. This is spiritual listening, and quiet is the sound of Jesus connecting with your soul, not your conscious mind. Remember that your

subconscious mind is working, and your spirit is responding whether you are conscious of it or not.

Don't forget to be patient and cut yourself some slack. If there is a lot of noise in your head, try using your "sacred word" or a phrase from a favorite song to call yourself back from the chaos!

Week 3 Headline:

An Enemy Attempts a Takeover But Fails

I can't really imagine Jesus meeting with Satan. How could Jesus stand being around the one who had seemingly ruined His creation? Jesus describes their meeting alone in the wilderness. He has officially stepped into His Messianic role after His baptism and now faces His formidable foe for the first time perhaps since the Garden of Eden. Satan, who has enjoyed free reign over creation and humanity, now faces the Messiah, who is ready to launch His mission to free humanity from spiritual exile.

It begins as a war of words. Jesus uses this encounter with Satan to establish that He is qualified to lead humanity out of the wilderness. He submits His human need for provision and protection to the gracious nature of His Father. He submits His divine right to dominion over creation to the authority of the one true God.

I love it! The tide is already turning in the story of the global disaster caused by man. The victory over sin and Satan has begun as Jesus overcomes the direct challenge of Satan for control of creation, the "promised land" for humanity. The failure of a rebellious Israel is no longer a barrier to the restoration of God's people. This opens the door for the promises and blessings soon to come through Jesus.

Before You Meet:

Spend some time familiarizing yourself with the story you will be investigating. Read Luke 4:1-15, Mark 1:12-15, and Matthew 4:1-11. A quick read through Deuteronomy 6 will help give you an idea of the Jewish context for this story.

To Begin Your Meeting:

Read this week's headline and then Matthew 4:1-11 out loud. Invite Jesus to join you to help answer some questions, and thankfully acknowledge that His

Spirit is present as your Helper to guide your discussion. Please do not let this become some kind of ritual prayer. Remember, it is an actual invitation.

To Begin Your Discussion:

Read the following introduction out loud to the group:

Soon after being identified as the chosen Messiah, Jesus encounters a familiar enemy. Remember, Jesus first confronted Satan in the famous Garden of Eden (Genesis 3:14-15). This time, the slimy, abysmal deceiver of mankind approaches the newly appointed Messiah while alone in the wilderness in an attempt to ensnare Him. It seems the fate of the new Kingdom is only one choice away from failure. How does Jesus avoid a repeat of the tragic choice made by Adam and Eve in the Garden?

Discuss the following questions one at a time.

Read each question out loud and listen to what each person is saying. Ask questions to clarify and develop ideas together as a group. Help each other stay on topic with the reminder, "What does this have to do with the question we are discussing?"

1. Why do the biographers focus our attention on three final, specific temptations— regarding God's provision, protection, and power—in the wilderness? What might the disciples have realized about the parallels in their nation's history of failure to avoid temptation?

2. As His defense against Satan's lies, Jesus refers to Moses' familiar message to the nation of Israel as it was coming out of the wilderness (this message is recorded in Deuteronomy). Someone read Hebrews 3:7-11 for comparison. What kind of heart did Jesus have that the nation of Israel did not?

3. Why is this encounter with Satan significant as the prelude to the launch of a new spiritual Kingdom?

4. How does this story affect *our* opportunity to be a part of a new Kingdom story?

Note some of the ideas that strike you as especially meaningful:

Before you leave, share one or two of these ideas with the group. Read back important highlights from the previous weeks and add ideas from the current discussion. It is essential that you take a few minutes to do this before you break up the meeting. Continue circulating the notes. Use your text group or other social media tools to raise additional questions for further discussion but try not to get too far off the main subject. Don't forget that keeping a journal for yourself is also helpful.

Close with a prayer of thanksgiving and expectation that God will continue to show you more.

Within a day or two of your discussion, take at least one 15-minute time-out to allow Jesus to have easy access to your heart.

Sit comfortably, close your eyes, with no phone, no Bible, and no notepad. This is a time for you to just be in the presence of Jesus. Always begin by inviting the Holy Spirit to speak. Let thoughts go past you as you use this as sacred time with God. This is spiritual listening, and quiet is the sound of Jesus connecting with your soul, not your conscious mind. Remember that your

subconscious mind is working, and your spirit is responding, whether you are conscious of it or not.

Don't forget to be patient and cut yourself some slack. If there is a lot of noise in your head, try using your "sacred word" or the phrase of a special song to call yourself back from the chaos!

Week 4 Headline:

Jesus Begins the March to Freedom for the World

I wish Jesus would have just snapped His fingers to solve our problem. Instead, He begins the hard work of reaching the lost, one person at a time. As prophesied years before, the Kingdom of God would indeed come from the nation of Israel, but Jesus shows the wounded and enslaved people of the world that they would have to follow Him to escape.

Jesus intentionally chooses a group of twelve totally undeserving disciples, just as His Father had chosen the tribe of Jacob and His twelve sons to represent Himself to the world. Through a series of stories, we see how Jesus brings healing and joy to those who have faith, regardless of race or status, education or family line. We see Jesus' domain penetrating the everyday world as well as places of power, darkness, and religious intolerance.

I love how this story unfolds! The march to freedom and God's blessing for all creation has begun. But clearly there is a mixed response to Jesus. The stories also show the grief and loss of those who do not have faith and repentance. Satan has not given up and continues to deceive and blind those who are lost in the wilderness. By turning the political and religious powers against Jesus, Satan makes a final attempt to hold onto his old domain.

Before You Meet:

Spend some time familiarizing yourself with the story you will be investigating. Read Matthew 8–10. It's a long section of Scripture with lots of great information, but you only need to focus on the variety of characters in the stories.

To Begin Your Meeting:

Read this week's headline and then the chapter subtitles found in Matthew 8–10 out loud. (You may have to find a version that has subtitles!) Remember that these titles are not in the original Bible but are added in many translations to help you quickly navigate the stories found in the Gospels. Invite Jesus to join you to help answer some questions, and thankfully acknowledge that His Spirit is present as your Helper to guide your discussion. Please do not let this become some kind of ritual prayer. Remember, it is an actual invitation.

To Begin Your Discussion:

Read the following introduction out loud to the group:

After accepting His role as God's chosen Messiah and establishing His authority to lead His followers out of the metaphorical wilderness, Jesus directs His attention to the people of His day-to-day world. Why does the story of Jesus seem to unfold so slowly, one person at a time? Surely all He has to do is take control. But that is not His way. It seems Jesus must first show the world *how* to follow Him out of the wilderness.

Discuss the Following Questions One at a Time.

Read each question out loud and listen to what each person is saying. Ask questions to clarify and develop ideas together as a group. Help each other stay on topic with the reminder, "What does this have to do with the question we are discussing?"

1. Jesus clearly invites everyone to follow Him, so why does He specifically choose twelve Jewish disciples. Why does He choose them *at the beginning* of his ministry, and what do they represent?

2. How do the biographers use stories of personal healing to prove that the Kingdom of heaven has come—as promised by the prophets of Israel? Someone read Isaiah 61:1 and Luke 4:18-19 for more information.

3. Why do the biographers use such a great diversity of people and places to tell the Good News of God's Kingdom come?

4. What is the big picture in this grouping of stories? And why is it important for us?

Note some of the ideas that strike you as especially meaningful:

Before you leave, share one or two of these ideas with the group. Read back important highlights from the previous week and add ideas from the current discussion. It is essential that you take a few minutes to do this before you break up the meeting. Continue circulating the notes. Use your text group or other social media tools to raise additional questions for further discussion but try not to get too far off the main subject. Don't forget that keeping a journal for yourself is also helpful.

Close with a prayer of thanksgiving and expectation that God will continue to show you more.

Within a day or two of your discussion, take at least one 15-minute time-out to allow Jesus to have easy access to your heart.

Sit comfortably, close your eyes, with no phone, no Bible, and no notepad. This is a time for you to just be in the presence of Jesus. Always begin by inviting the Holy Spirit to speak. Let thoughts go past you as you use this as sacred time with God. This is spiritual listening, and quiet is the sound of Jesus connecting with your soul, not your conscious mind. Remember that your

subconscious mind is working, and your spirit is responding whether you are conscious of it or not.

Don't forget to be patient and cut yourself some slack. If there is a lot of noise in your head, try using your "sacred word" or the phrase of a favorite song to call yourself back from the chaos!

Week 5 Headline:

A Meeting with Some Ancient Prophets Marks a Changing of the Guard

---

I am not sure what I would have thought or felt if I was there to see Moses and Elijah show up. Maybe that's why Jesus brought only His closest disciples with Him. As momentum builds towards the final episodes in Jesus' ministry, they literally see Jesus encounter the long-dead mediators of the ancient agreement between God and Israel (referred to as the Old Covenant). The disciples did not understand it at the time, but in retrospect, Jesus was beginning the final leg of His journey with a sort of "handoff" from those who literally "wrote the book" on the Old Covenant (i.e., Moses and Elijah)!

Jesus is "transfigured" to reveal His true heavenly calling as a *new Moses* to lead a *new people* with *new hearts* to a *new Kingdom*. The heavenly Father audibly endorses His Son as His final and complete solution for man. As the beloved royal Son, Jesus will lead His people to a new promised land. But unlike the terms of the old agreement under Moses and Elijah that resulted in death, Jesus will initiate a new and better agreement between God and man—one that brings eternal Life.

I find it a little strange that the Creator—God Himself—would bother to make any kind of agreement with us. But such is the love God has for those created in His image. The battle for the restoration of humanity required the initiation of a new agreement between God and a new mediator for all mankind—Jesus. The disciples slowly came to understand the promise of a New Covenant, which would transform hearts (Jeremiah 31:31). They ultimately realized that Jesus was the mediator of this new agreement (Hebrews 9:11-14) and that He was given the authority to make it happen.

I have to laugh a bit when I think of Peter running around, trying to build a few tents for these famous people. It would take him a while to realize that the tabernacles where God dwelt during the years of wandering in the wilderness under the Old Covenant were now a thing of the past. Humanity had a new agreement with the Creator. Under the terms of this New Covenant, the power of the Holy Spirit could now dwell within us to change hearts and restore Life. All it required was faith in Jesus, the Author of the agreement!

Before You Meet:

Spend some time familiarizing yourself with the story you will be investigating. Read Luke 9:28-36, Mark 9:1-13, Matthew 17:1-13, Luke 16:16, and 2 Peter 1:16-21. Some Old Testament reading will be helpful as well. Read Exodus 34:29-35, Jeremiah 31:31-34, and Malachi 4:4-5. I suggest reading this story in several Gospel accounts to give you a more complete picture. The connections with the Old Testament are stunning!

To Begin Your Meeting:

Read this week's headline and then Mark 9:1-13 out loud. Invite Jesus to join you to help answer some questions, and thankfully acknowledge that His Spirit is present as your Helper to guide your discussion. Please do not let this become some kind of ritual prayer. Remember, it is an actual invitation.

To Begin Your Discussion:

Read the following introduction out loud to the group:

Jesus invites a few of His disciples to a very strange meeting. It had been 400 years since anyone in Israel had seen a prophet. Needless to say, the disciples are confused when they see Jesus meeting with *two* long-dead prophets, Moses and Elijah. How did the disciples recognize them? We don't know. But we do know what Jesus, Moses, and Elijah were discussing, and that Jesus was noticeably changed by the encounter in a way reminiscent of Moses' radiant encounter with God on Mount Sinai. What is going on in what seems like a bizarre ghost story?

Discuss the Following Questions One at a Time.

Read each question out loud and listen to what each person is saying. Ask questions to clarify and develop ideas together as a group. Help each other stay on topic with the reminder, "What does this have to do with the question we are discussing?"

1. What do Moses and Elijah each represent to the disciples? It may be helpful to have someone read Malachi 4:4-5. (Note, this is the last book in the Old Testament.)

2. How could Jesus and His commandments become the fulfillment of the Law and the Prophets? It may be helpful to take a moment to read Matthew 22:37-40 and Luke 16:16.

3. Why are the prophets discussing Jesus' "departure"? Someone read Luke 9:31 for more information. Why does Peter want to build tabernacles (tents) for them? Keep in mind that the word used here is literally "exodus," which carries a double meaning of completion and physical departure.

4. Remember how Moses' face was shining after being face-to-face with God in the cloud on Mount Sinai? Now the appearance of Jesus shines. How might this story mark a change in the spiritual domain? And why does this story matter to us now?

Note some of the ideas that strike you as especially meaningful:

Before you leave, share one or two of these ideas with the group. Read back important highlights from the previous week and add ideas from the current discussion. It is essential that you take a few minutes to do this before you break up the meeting. Continue circulating the notes. Use your text group or other social media tools to raise additional questions for further discussion but try not to get too far off the main subject. Don't forget that keeping a journal for yourself is also helpful.

Close with a prayer of thanksgiving and expectation that God will continue to show you more.

Within a day or two of your discussion, take at least one 15-minute time-out to allow Jesus to have easy access to your heart.

Sit comfortably, close your eyes, with no phone, no Bible, and no notepad. This is a time for you to just be in the presence of Jesus. Always begin by inviting the Holy Spirit to speak. Let thoughts go past you as you use this as sacred time with God. This is spiritual listening, and quiet is the sound of Jesus connecting with your soul, not your conscious mind. Remember that your subconscious mind is working, and your spirit is responding whether you are conscious of it or not.

Don't forget to be patient and cut yourself some slack. If there is a lot of noise in your head, try using your "sacred word" or a phrase from a favorite song to call yourself back from the chaos!

Week 6 Headline:

An Ancient Curse on Humanity is Broken

I find it difficult to fully understand the death of Jesus. The facts are clear enough—a harsh injustice leads to a miserable death at the hands of a religious establishment that uses Rome to do its dirty work. My problem is wrapping my head around the real story here. I can see justice at work. But shouldn't I also see the immense spiritual powers at play? What if this isn't simply a case of God balancing the cosmic scales of justice?

Let's consider another point of view. In the most severe and final test of His willingness to submit to His Father, Jesus yields Himself to the power of death and the curse of the law by being lifted up on the cross (Deuteronomy 21:22-23, Galatians 3:13). He experiences the fullness of the pain and loss that have resulted from the ancient curse placed on humanity by the Creator in the Garden of Eden (Genesis 3:14-18). The same God who announced to all creation that the human beings He created were very good—the One who placed the creatures made in His image over the rest of creation—this same Creator also pronounced a spiritual curse that took away our birthright and left us to experience the consequences of our choice to do things our own way.

Jesus experienced the curse of sin as a man without sin—as One who wholly submitted Himself to God. The result is that the tables were turned in the spiritual realm, resulting in Satan's self-defeat. Death would no longer be a weapon of Satan; it would now be the power of God for the salvation of humanity (1 Corinthians 1:18). By submissively giving up His innocent life, Jesus would open once and for all the only possible door leading to the promise of blessing and rest (shalom). The pathway to Life would be cleared of all barriers for all who walk by faith.

There is quite a bit more I could say about all this. But let me end my reflections with a thought to challenge you. In the context of the Passover imagery of the Last Supper story, the death of Jesus tells us that we have been released from our spiritual slavery to Satan and have been placed under a New Covenant agreement with God. We no longer live under the authority of a curse that separates us from our Creator; we live under the promise of the love of God being poured into our hearts. Release from the curse means payment is no longer necessary! That's the point!

The story of Jesus' crucifixion is far more than payment for sin. It is the foundation of an incredible love story of a Lamb given by God (John 1:29) to secure our freedom from slavery by eliminating the claim of our enslaver—by declaring it null and void so that we can begin a journey to a new Kingdom. (This is, of course, a reminder of the lamb that God provided in the story of Abraham and Isaac in Genesis 22.) Only the disloyal and faithless (like Judas) remain lost. But as John says, "This is how God shows His love for the world in that He gave His one and only Son so that everyone who believes in Him won't be lost to evil but will be restored to the fullness of Life that the Creator always intended" (John 3:16, my paraphrase).

Before You Meet:

Spend some time familiarizing yourself with the story you will be investigating. Read Matthew 27:1-66, Luke 23:1-56, Mark 15:1-47, and John 19:1-42. I think you will find it helpful to see this story from the various points of view that each Gospel writer brings out. In addition, it would be worth taking some additional time to read Matthew 26:20- 29, Mark 14:22-25, Luke 22:14-23, and John 13–17 to get an idea of the context for this story. For a look at how the story was retold by the early church in a sacramental form, see 1 Corinthians 11:23-26. I know it's a lot of reading but well worth it!

To Begin Your Meeting:

Read this week's headline and then Matthew 27:1-66 out loud. Invite Jesus to join you to help answer some questions, and thankfully acknowledge that His Spirit is present as your Helper to guide your discussion. Please do not let this become some kind of ritual prayer. Remember, it is an actual invitation.

To Begin Your Discussion:

Read the following introduction out loud to the group:

Having failed using a direct approach, Satan must now find another way to maintain supremacy. He bases his lethal strategy on the hardness of human hearts and the ease with which he can manipulate human desires. Deception and death are Satan's ultimate weapons, and he believes he can use Jesus' passion for the Truth as a weapon against Him. Jesus comes face-to-face with the worst of human nature as He experiences betrayal, abandonment, and injustice. But Jesus endures the resulting humiliation and pain on His final journey to the cross with confidence in a deeper Truth, unknown to Satan at the time.

The story of Jesus' sacrifice is probably the most familiar and personally impactful of all the stories of Jesus. But what does this story tell us about the deep realities of the spiritual realm? Is this only a story of heroism, or is it also the story of Satan's self-defeat? Is this some cosmic scale of justice balanced by an innocent death, or is it the power of evil exposed as a deception and completely exhausted?

Discuss the Following Questions One at a Time.

Read each question out loud and listen to what each person is saying. Ask questions to clarify and develop ideas together as a group. Help each other stay on topic with the reminder, "What does this have to do with the question we are discussing?"

1. Why is it important that this particular story is played out in the context of the Passover feast?

2. Why do the biographers seem intent for us to know that Jesus' death is both voluntary *and* sinless?

3. Was it even possible for Jesus to die of natural causes? Why is it necessary for Him to submit Himself to death?

4. How do you see the sacrificial death of Jesus? Was it a payment to an angry God, or a victory by a loving God over the power of the curse of the law? Why does it matter to us today?

Note some of the ideas that strike you as especially meaningful:

Before you leave, share one or two of these ideas with the group. Read back important highlights from the previous week and add ideas from the current discussion. It is essential that you take a few minutes to do this before you break up the meeting. Continue circulating the notes. Use your text group or other social media tools to raise additional questions for further discussion but try not to get too far off the main subject. Don't forget that keeping a journal for yourself is also helpful.

Close with a prayer of thanksgiving and expectation that God will continue to show you more.

Within a day or two of your discussion, take at least one 15-minute time-out to allow Jesus to have easy access to your heart.

Sit comfortably, close your eyes, with no phone, no Bible, and no notepad. This is a time for you to just be in the presence of Jesus. Always begin by inviting the Holy Spirit to speak. Let thoughts go past you as you use this as sacred time with God. This is spiritual listening, and quiet is the sound of Jesus connecting with your soul, not your conscious mind. Remember that your subconscious mind is working, and your spirit is responding, whether you are conscious of it or not.

Don't forget to be patient and cut yourself some slack. If there is a lot of noise in your head, try using your "sacred word" or a phrase from a favorite song to call yourself back from the chaos!

Week 7 Headline:

A Resurrection Restores the Power of Life

Easter has always been my favorite holiday. Christmas is fun and, of course, quite special. But Easter is, well, special-er! I still cry singing hymns and songs about the resurrection. The story of a new beginning for humanity reaches a climax as Jesus comes out of the grave with a new kind of human body. A new sort of Life could now flow back into the world—a resurrected Life that for the first time since the fall in the Garden is free from sin and death. In fulfillment of all the prophecies about Him and His own predictions, Jesus experiences the power of His Father to create Life. Incredible!

The followers of Jesus would soon learn that He was just the first to be fully outfitted for eternal Life. The curse placed on humanity in the Garden of Eden, which separated us from the Creator (a curse amplified by the curse of the law), was finally and forever broken. Death had no hold on those who place their faith in Jesus. The expansion of the Kingdom of God could now proceed. Jesus paved the way for a new set of promises to be fulfilled in and through His followers. The transformation of human hearts is now made possible by the same power that raised Jesus from the dead.

I love to imagine the gravestone rolled back, the angelic beings attending an empty grave, and the stunned disciples standing in disbelief. And I picture the Divine Gardener once again strolling in the garden waiting to meet His Father and calling a young woman by name, making it clear she is still very much a part of His Life. The resurrected Jesus would be returning to His heavenly home with a few costly scars but with victory in hand for us all.

Before You Meet:

Spend some time familiarizing yourself with the story you will be investigating. Read Matthew 28:1-20, Mark 16:1-8, Luke 24:1-49, Acts 1:3-8, and John 20:1-29. I include references here from all four Gospel writers to give you as much detail as possible about this incredible event.

To Begin Your Meeting:

Read this week's headline and then Matthew 28:1-20 out loud. Invite Jesus to join you to help answer some questions, and thankfully acknowledge that His Spirit is present as your Helper to guide your discussion. Please do not let this become some kind of ritual prayer. Remember, it is an actual invitation.

To Begin Your Discussion:

Read the following introduction out loud to the group:

Jesus' death was clearly not the end—it was a beginning! He experiences the life-giving power of God His Father for more than His own vindication—indeed, to create a new hope for humanity! The story is like a grand finale in the ministry of Jesus. But why is this not the end of our story?

Discuss the Following Questions One at a Time.

Read each question out loud and listen to what each person is saying. Ask questions to clarify and develop ideas together as a group. Help each other stay on topic with the reminder, "What does this have to do with the question we are discussing?"

1. Why do the biographers seem to emphasize that Jesus is still human after His resurrection?

2. How is the resurrection of Jesus different than other resurrections, like that of Lazarus?

3. What does Jesus' resurrection represent? Someone read Matthew 27:52-53 and consider the implications.

4. How does life change for the followers of Jesus in the first 40 days after His resurrection? Someone read Romans 8:11. How does our story today change because of the resurrection of Jesus?

Note some of the ideas that strike you as especially meaningful:

Before you leave, share one or two of these ideas with the group. Read back important highlights from the previous week and add ideas from the current discussion. It is essential that you take a few minutes to do this before you break up the meeting. Continue circulating the notes. Use your text group or other social media tools to raise additional questions for further discussion but try not to get too far off the main subject. Don't forget that keeping a journal for yourself is also helpful.

Close with a prayer of thanksgiving and expectation that God will continue to show you more.

Within a day or two of your discussion, take at least one 15-minute time-out to allow Jesus to have easy access to your heart.

Sit comfortably, close your eyes, with no phone, no Bible, and no notepad. This is a time for you to just be in the presence of Jesus. Always begin by inviting the Holy Spirit to speak. Let thoughts go past you as you use this as sacred time with God. This is spiritual listening, and quiet is the sound of Jesus connecting with your soul, not your conscious mind. Remember that your subconscious mind is working, and your spirit is responding whether you are conscious of it or not.

Don't forget to be patient and cut yourself some slack. If there is a lot of noise in your head, try using your "sacred word" or the phrase of a favorite song to call yourself back from the chaos!

Week 8 Headline:

A Human King Sits on the Throne of God

To me, it's a rather abrupt ending to the events of Jesus' life. No farewell party. No pats on the back. No reminiscing about all the great miracles seen. For the disciples, the ascension of Jesus is the final event in their time together. They quickly learn that the ascension of Jesus closes a chapter but doesn't end the book.

The launch of the Kingdom of God is almost complete. The curse is broken, a new agreement between God and man has been ratified, the power of death has been overcome, and a new kind of Life is possible, pouring like rivers of water out of Jesus by His Spirit. All that is left to do before His physical departure is to hand off His mission to His followers. They must continue His work in the *seen* realm as He rules from the *unseen.*

The events take place on the Mount of Olives. It was here that Jesus prayed for His cup of suffering to pass, perhaps reminiscent of His ancestor David's mournful prayer in this same place (2 Samuel 15:23). It was here that His ride into Jerusalem began, and where, just a few days later, He experienced the betrayal leading to His death (Matthew 21:1-11 and 26:30-56). It was here that Jesus taught His disciples what lay ahead for them (Matthew 24–25), even as He anticipated His return to this exact spot sometime in the future (Zechariah 14:14). To complete His journey on earth, Jesus only need pass from the realm of this world into the unseen realm of heaven through the thin veil that now separates them! He does so at the exact spot to which He will return.

His command to the disciples to carry on is bittersweet. He explains that He needs to leave physically so He can be present everywhere spiritually. Jesus "ascended" to a throne at His Father's right hand, but we should be encouraged that this is not some distant heavenly domain. We now enjoy His Presence by experiencing the work of the Holy Spirit in our lives, using His authority to expand His Kingdom and the power of His resurrection to pour Life into others. Because of this Presence, the completion of the work of Jesus is assured.

I grew up in my faith with the simple idea that I must "live in light of the world to come." The ascension story makes sense of that idea. Jesus is formally installed as the victorious King of heaven and earth. He is seated on the throne at His Father's right hand to rule, waiting for His enemies to be made His footstool while we live in His forgiveness and relationship with Him (Hebrews 10:12-17). The Spirit of God is directed through us to expand the Kingdom that Jesus successfully launched. Jesus awaits the signal from His Father to physically return to the seen realm to finalize the transformation of heaven and earth.

Before You Meet:

Spend some time familiarizing yourself with the story you will be investigating. Read Matthew 28:16-20, Luke 24:50-53, Acts 1:6-12, John 20:19-23, and Colossians 3:1. All these references are important to get the full picture of how this story transitions to the story of the early church.

To Begin Your Meeting:

Read this week's headline and then Matthew 28:16-20 out loud. Invite Jesus to join you to help answer some questions, and thankfully acknowledge that His Spirit is present as your Helper to guide your discussion. Please do not let this become some kind of ritual prayer. Remember, it is an actual invitation.

To Begin Your Discussion:

Read the following introduction out loud to the group:

By His death, Jesus undid the curse resulting from the rebellion of humankind. By His resurrection, Jesus establishes resurrection Life as the new way forward for all who follow Him. But this did not totally end the conflict with Satan. Victory is already secured, but skirmishes for control still continue at a practical and personal level. Jesus ascends to the throne as both Son of God and Son of Man, with a plan clearly in mind to continue the work He started. Did Jesus see humanity as part of His plan all along? Why not stay and finish what He started, now that He was humanly immortal (resurrected)?

Discuss the Following Questions One at a Time.

Read each question out loud and listen to what each person is saying. Ask questions to clarify and develop ideas together as a group. Help each other stay on topic with the reminder, "What does this have to do with the question we are discussing?"

1. How do the biographers paint the picture that Jesus was still with them even though He is now seated on His throne as King? Is this throne temporary or permanent?

2. Someone read Matthew 19:28 and Matthew 25:31. How does the ascension prove that the Kingdom of God was successfully launched?

3. What is our role in this new Kingdom?

4. What is it like for Jesus who now sits on the throne as our Priest and our King? Take a minute to read Hebrews 4:16, 8:1, 12:2, and Revelation 4:1-11 out loud.

Note some of the ideas that strike you as especially meaningful.

Before you leave, share one or two of these ideas with the group. Read back important highlights from the previous week and add ideas from the current discussion. It is essential that you take a few minutes to do this before you break up the meeting. Continue circulating the notes. Use your text group or other social media tools to raise additional questions for further discussion but try not to get too far off the main subject. Don't forget that keeping a journal for yourself is also helpful.

Close with a prayer of thanksgiving and expectation that God will continue to show you more.

Within a day or two of your discussion, take at least one 15-minute time-out to allow Jesus to have easy access to your heart.

Sit comfortably, close your eyes, with no phone, no Bible, and no notepad. This is a time for you to just be in the presence of Jesus. Always begin by inviting the Holy Spirit to speak. Let thoughts go past you as you use this as sacred time with God. This is spiritual listening, and quiet is the sound of Jesus connecting with your soul, not your conscious mind. Remember that your subconscious mind is working, and your spirit is responding whether you are conscious of it or not.

Don't forget to be patient and cut yourself some slack. If there is a lot of noise in your head, try using your "sacred word" or phrase from a special song to call yourself back from the chaos!

Digging Deeper Into The Story Of Jesus

Key question:

How do the events in the ministry of Jesus tell the story of a new starting point for humanity? Why do we now have choices that can truly change our future?

Discuss this Statement:

An act of creation power by God the Father paves the way for a new set of promises to be fulfilled in and through the followers of King Jesus as they are transformed by the same power that raised Him from the dead. It was not just a change in a relationship with God—it was a new Life for those who chose to follow Him.

To Prepare for Your Next Part of this Series:

Consider the following questions: What would it be like for us today if the biographies of Jesus included only the events and none of His teachings? What would be missing? Isn't it enough to simply know that Jesus died and rose again?

Part 2

Digging deeper into the teachings of Jesus.

Feature Story #2:
A Path to Restoration Revealed

How Jesus reveals His ultimate purpose.

Welcome to Part 2 of your guide through the Gospels! I hope you are excited to come back for more. The first Feature Story in *The Importance of Embracing Jesus* covered the new starting point for humanity as revealed by key events in Jesus' life. This series will now guide you through His revolutionary teachings and examples. Jesus' life was more than just a series of spiritually significant events—His ministry was rich with wisdom! Our two Feature Stories in this series will take you through what Jesus was saying that stirred the crowds and transformed a group of unlikely disciples.

Jesus was well aware that people needed some help figuring out how to move forward with the life they lived under strict Roman and religious rule. His radical messages provide the Truth they needed to challenge the cultural rules. I would say that key events of Jesus' life are inspiring enough even without His teachings. But when you include His teachings, the picture of the Creator's long-awaited plan to restore humanity and the world becomes personal and powerful! It's much bigger than politics or religion. Your job in Part 2 is to dig deeper into these teachings.

Our primary source for Feature Story #2 will be the Gospel of Matthew. He was one of the disciples who experienced a transformational process in his own life. Levi the tax collector became Matthew the student, who then became Matthew the teacher, and finally Matthew the martyr! He writes from the point of view of an outsider finding his way inside a fellowship of people called to restore Life to the world through the message of Jesus. As a source for your investigation, his Gospel not only informs, but also invites you into this inner circle of followers! Your job will take you inside that inner circle to explore how the path to restoration is revealed.

Uniquely written some years after Jesus' ascension, the Gospel of Matthew is what I would call an orientation guide for those who wanted to follow Jesus, the enthroned King of a new spiritual domain on earth. It contains key teachings that were put together to guide novice followers of Jesus the Rabbi to a mature relationship with Jesus the King. As you discuss the teachings, pay particular attention to how Matthew shows Jesus communicating cross-culturally and cross-generationally. Sometimes we see Jesus speaking to His inner circle and sometimes to large crowds. Matthew is the perfect source to expose the ultimate purpose for what Jesus did. Enjoy your discussions!

Week 1 Headline:

The Path To Restoration Begins With A New Blessing

The Sermon on the Mount (Matthew 5–7) was the first section of Scripture I memorized as a young teenager. I remember sitting in the back seat of our car practicing it over and over again on a long family road trip. In fact, by the time we finished our twelve-hour drive, I had memorized the whole sermon! There was something about the Beatitudes that was particularly mesmerizing. Here, Jesus announces the blessing of God to those marginalized by society—the poor, the meek, and the broken. According to the opening lines of His sermon, the blessing of Abraham—once the exclusive right of the Kingdom of Israel—now belonged to a much more inclusive Kingdom of Heaven. This new Kingdom did not belong to the religious elite or the wealthy. A new blessing was reserved for those who hungered for righteousness and who were willing to seek peace with their fellow man—regardless of their heritage or religious background.

Something about these words gave me hope. In His radical opening remarks of this sermon, Jesus made it clear that all who seek the Kingdom of God will find the Kingdom of God! Sickness, poverty, and grief do not keep you out—they actually prepare you for the blessings of the Kingdom! This was exactly what Isaiah had prophesied long ago (Isaiah 61:1-3). God's plan all along was that His blessings would be poured out on all who were ready to receive them. I couldn't help but feel these words were for me.

Before You Meet:

Spend some time familiarizing yourself with the teaching you will be investigating. Read Matthew 5:1-16. Compare this with Isaiah 61:1-3 for additional background.

To Begin Your Meeting:

Read this week's headline and then Matthew 5:1-16 out loud. Invite Jesus to join you and answer some questions. Thankfully acknowledge that His Spirit is present as your Helper to guide your discussion. I will remind you to do this each week. Please do not let this become some kind of ritual prayer. Remember, it is an actual invitation.

To Begin Your Discussion:

Read the following introduction out loud to the group:

John the Baptist has been arrested, and Jesus is becoming infamous in the outer regions of Israel as He heals the sick and preaches the coming of His Kingdom. Jesus has chosen a few men from various backgrounds to be His students, but He is also attracting attention as well as followers from the disenfranchised and the desperate in most of the major cities, including various Jewish sects and Gentiles. This unusual group of people follow Him to a hillside near the Sea of Galilee to hear more. Jesus is a long way from Jerusalem, the center of religious teaching, but here He delivers His first and perhaps His most famous sermon.

Discuss the Following Questions One at a Time.

Read each question out loud and listen to what each person is saying. Ask questions to clarify and develop ideas together as a group. Help each other stay on topic with the reminder, "What does this have to do with the question we are discussing?"

1. What sort of people were in the audience for this sermon?

2. In what ways did these particular Jews fail to meet the religious standard for receiving the blessing of Abraham?

3. According to Jesus, who was actually qualified to receive the blessings that Israel expected to receive?

4. What was so different about the Kingdom of Heaven?

Note some of the ideas that strike you as especially meaningful:

Before you leave, share one or two of these ideas with the group. Read back important highlights from the previous week and add ideas from the current discussion. It is essential that you take a few minutes to do this before you break up the meeting. Circulate the notes. Use your text group or other social media tools to raise additional questions for further discussion but try not to get too far off the main subject. Don't forget that keeping a journal for yourself may also be helpful.

Close with a prayer of thanksgiving and expectation that God will continue to show you more.

Within a day or two of your discussion, take at least one 15-minute time-out to allow Jesus to have easy access to your heart.

Sit comfortably, close your eyes, with no phone, no Bible, and no notepad. This is a time for you to just be in the presence of Jesus. Always begin by inviting the Holy Spirit to speak. His is a Voice with no words. Let thoughts go past you as you use this as sacred time with God. This is spiritual listening, and quiet is the sound of Jesus connecting with your soul, not your conscious mind.

Remember that your subconscious mind is working, and your spirit is responding whether you are conscious of it or not.

If this is your first time to try spiritual "listening," please review Appendix 2 as an orientation. Don't forget to be patient and cut yourself some slack. If there is a lot of noise in your head, try using a single word to reduce the clutter. Some people find that a familiar song can be helpful. With time, you may find a "sacred word" that is very personal to you. Don't focus on the word—just use it to call yourself back from the chaos!

Week 2 Headline:

The Path to Human Greatness

It seems to me that "the Law" as given by God was something quite beautiful. So simple, but elegant in its moral clarity and consistency. It has stood the test of time as a basis for justice and democracy around the world. The problem was that the Law of Moses, intended to bring blessing to the world, had become a source of national pride and isolation for Israel. Jesus shows His Jewish audience that the intended purpose of their law (it's "fulfillment") is to produce humility of heart, not just submission of the will. Jesus emphasizes that God's purpose was not to empower the righteous but rather to encourage all people to greatness in His Kingdom.

Jesus chooses five specific laws of Israel to paint a picture of the deep social issues that kept them from becoming what God intended them to be as a nation. First, they should have seen that murder was not a moral issue, hate is. Instead of quickly seeking reconciliation, they allowed anger to escalate to the point of murder. Second, the nation should have realized that adultery was not a moral issue, lust is. They allow it to invade their whole body and even justify promiscuity with illegal divorce. Third, a misspoken oath was not a moral issue, failure to do what you say is. The cultural traditions in Israel encouraged people to only mean what they say in certain conditions rather than speaking with integrity in all circumstances.

Fourth, and especially relevant in our world today, Jesus makes it clear that a culture based on vengeance and *individual* rights will never really achieve social justice. This can only be achieved when individuals see others having the same rights as they do. In addition, Jesus challenges Israel's religious nationalism that isolates rather than blesses others. He makes it clear that the only hope for justice and blessing is love that embraces all, even our enemies. Seems like a good reminder!

I love the deeper perspective on morality given by Jesus. Seeking reconciliation with others, exercising self-control, speaking with integrity, maintaining social equality, and expressing love to all—all of these potentially bring out a greatness in us that following the letter of the law cannot. Jesus wasn't trying to make us feel like a hopeless mess. He just wanted His followers to avoid hiding behind shallow obedience!

Before You Meet:

Spend some time familiarizing yourself with the teaching you will be investigating. Read Matthew 5:13-48. It will be helpful to compare these verses with Luke 6:17-49.

To Begin Your Meeting:

Read this week's headline and then Matthew 5:13-48 out loud. Invite Jesus to join you and answer some questions. Thankfully acknowledge that His Spirit is present as your Helper to guide your discussion. Please do not let this become some kind of ritual prayer. Remember, it is an actual invitation.

To Begin Your Discussion:

Read the following introduction out loud to the group:

Jesus continues with His Sermon on the Mount by revealing the real meaning of the Torah (the first five books of the Old Testament). Each time Jesus says, "You have heard it said, but I say to you . . ." His audience must sense His indictment of the religious leaders and teachers of His day. Jesus seems to raise the bar on what was already hard enough! Why was Jesus setting a new standard that was even further out of reach?

Discuss the following questions one at a time.

Read each question out loud and listen to what each person is saying. Ask questions to clarify and develop ideas together as a group. Help each other stay on topic with the reminder, "What does this have to do with the question we are discussing?"

1. Why was the Law (the Torah) so important to the Kingdom of Israel? You might look at Deuteronomy 30:9-30 if you are not sure about this one.

2. How does Jesus summarize the real purpose of the Law of Israel in Matthew 5:13-16, and why is this purpose important for His message about the new Kingdom of Heaven (Matthew 5:17-20)?

3. In Matthew 5:21-48 Jesus teaches on five specific topics in the Law. Why does Jesus choose these five in particular?

4. What clues does this teaching give us about God's heart for humanity? Why does He show us a way to greatness?

Note some of the ideas that strike you as especially meaningful:

Before you leave, share one or two of these ideas with the group. Read back important highlights from the previous week and add ideas from the current discussion. It is essential that you take a few minutes to do this before you break up the meeting. Continue circulating the notes. Use your text group or other social media tools to raise additional questions for further discussion but try not to get too far off the main subject. Don't forget that keeping a journal for yourself is also helpful.

Close with a prayer of thanksgiving and expectation that God will continue to show you more.

Within a day or two of your discussion, take at least one 15-minute time-out to allow Jesus to have easy access to your heart.

Sit comfortably, close your eyes, with no phone, no Bible, and no notepad. This is a time for you to just be in the presence of Jesus. Always begin by inviting the Holy Spirit to speak. Let thoughts go past you as you use this as sacred time with God. This is spiritual listening, and quiet is the sound of Jesus connecting with your soul, not your conscious mind. Remember that your subconscious mind is working, and your spirit is responding whether you are conscious of it or not.

Don't forget to be patient and cut yourself some slack. If there is a lot of noise in your head, try using your "sacred word" or phrase of a special song to call yourself back from the chaos!

Week 3 Headline:

The Path To Genuine Spirituality

I am the sort who prefers to be told what to do to succeed rather than having to guess. Generally, I am happy to comply with following the rules needed to get me what I want. But Jesus knew that the checklist approach to spirituality would lead to pride.

The religious life of the Jews had been corrupted by this sort of pride. With the Kingdom of heaven now at hand on earth, Jesus teaches his audience that this new spiritual Kingdom could not be experienced in the religious life they knew. A new approach to spirituality was needed to experience the full benefit of a new Kingdom.

Jesus discusses three fundamentals of religious practice needed for full spiritual development. First, instead of outward benevolence, Jesus teaches generosity of heart. Second, instead of praying flowery words, Jesus teaches communication with God. Third, instead of periodic fasting, Jesus teaches a life of humble restraint. Generosity, communication with God as a loving Father, and humble restraint were just what they needed to receive the rewards of a new spirituality. No checklist necessary.

I must point out that Jesus was careful to teach that all these practices are to be done "in secret" so that we don't make them into yet another religious exercise. But I think practicing these things in secret also proves that the real place of worship is in our hearts. The new Kingdom is no longer bound to activities in places of worship. Instead, rich spiritual reward is found in a relationship with the heavenly Father, anywhere, anytime.

Before You Meet:

Spend some time familiarizing yourself with the teaching which you will be investigating. Read Matthew 6:1-18. It is a short passage this week and worth reading several times.

To Begin Your Meeting:

Read this week's headline and then Matthew 6:1-18 out loud. Invite Jesus to join you and answer some questions. Thankfully acknowledge that His Spirit is present as your Helper to guide your discussion. Please do not let this become some kind of ritual prayer. Remember, it is an actual invitation.

To Begin Your Discussion:

Read the following introduction out loud to the group:

Jesus was on a roll! Having announced a new standard for blessing and how to achieve true greatness in His Kingdom, Jesus turns His attention to religious life. It seems that Jesus is quite prepared to shake His audience to the core by living a non-religious life. If religious life is not really sacred to Jesus, then what is?

Discuss the Following Questions One at a Time.

Read each question out loud and listen to what each person is saying. Ask questions to clarify and develop ideas together as a group. Help each other stay on topic with the reminder, "What does this have to do with the question we are discussing?"

1.   What was religious life like for the Jews at the time of Jesus?

2.   Of all the religious activities He could have chosen, why does Jesus choose these three specifically?

3.   How does Jesus try to restructure their existing religious practices into a spirituality that aligns with the new Kingdom of heaven on

earth? And why does Jesus say this will be rewarded by God Himself?

4.   What does Jesus' teaching imply we need to do today to change our religious practices into a heart for His Kingdom?

Note some of the ideas that strike you as especially meaningful:

Before you leave, share one or two of these ideas with the group. Read back important highlights from the previous week and add ideas from the current discussion. It is essential that you take a few minutes to do this before you break up the meeting. Continue circulating the notes. Use your text group or other social media tools to raise additional questions for further discussion but try not to get too far off the main subject. Don't forget that keeping a journal for yourself is also helpful.

Close with a prayer of thanksgiving and expectation that God will continue to show you more.

Within a day or two of your discussion, take at least one 15-minute time-out to allow Jesus to have easy access to your heart.

Sit comfortably, close your eyes, with no phone, no Bible, and no notepad. This is a time for you to just be in the presence of Jesus. Always begin by inviting the Holy Spirit to speak. Let thoughts go past you as you use this as sacred time with God. This is spiritual listening, and quiet is the sound of Jesus connecting with your soul, not your conscious mind. Remember that your

subconscious mind is working, and your spirit is responding whether you are conscious of it or not.

Don't forget to be patient and cut yourself some slack. If there is a lot of noise in your head, try using your "sacred word" or song phrase to call yourself back from the chaos!

Week 4 Headline:

The Path to True Freedom

I remember returning home after serving as a missionary surgeon in some of the poorest places on earth. One of our first stops was a Walmart. Within minutes, my wife and I ran out of the store completely overwhelmed. There was more food available for dogs than for many of our patients. And don't get me started on the sheer volume of junk! Jesus saw the obsession with material things in His day, too. At that time, heavy taxation (both political and religious) and the influence of Greek philosophies (Stoicism, Aestheticism, and Gnosticism) completely distorted the connections between the spiritual and material world. Those listening to Jesus were mostly uneducated and at the bottom of the social ladder, seeking relief from the consequences of a broken economic system.

Jesus tackles three economic topics to draw His audience back into a proper understanding of material things and to align their understanding with the reality of the new heavenly Kingdom He was offering. Each topic addresses a different driver of the broken economic system of their day. Jesus offers a radically different view based on the abundance found in His Kingdom.

First, Jesus teaches that the treasures of our world produce temporary security while the treasures of His Kingdom are eternal. Second, Jesus explains that the things that attract us in this world can also harm us while the things in His world produce Life out of an abundance of beauty and love. Finally, Jesus warns that the things we pursue out of fear and anxiety only add confusion and discord to our lives while the pursuit of the Kingdom provides all we need for peace and well-being.

I am not saying that there is something noble about being poor. Poverty and materialism *both* represent the failure of a purely physical world to meet our deepest needs. But Jesus taught that material and spiritual resources come together perfectly in the Kingdom of God! Our broken world teaches us we must produce wealth to survive while Jesus teaches us to receive from His abundance. Our system is driven by the need for accumulation and consumption; the Kingdom is built for daily satisfaction and wholeness.

I wonder what Jesus would think if He walked into a Walmart. In the context of the extraordinary wealth of the developed world, we must, more than ever, keep our eyes on this simple truth: The solution to the deep poverty that comes with having either too much or too little lies in the abundance of the Kingdom of heaven, not the redistribution or production of worldly wealth. I think Jesus would say He offers all the food, water, clothes, and shelter we really need on aisle Heaven. (Sorry, I just couldn't resist!)

Before You Meet:

Spend some time familiarizing yourself with the teaching you will be investigating. Read Matthew 6:19-34. Reread it several times so the words come easily. Try to get a sense of what it would be like to actually hear Jesus say the words.

To Begin Your Meeting:

Read this week's headline and then Matthew 6:19-34 out loud. Invite Jesus to join you and answer some questions. Thankfully acknowledge that His Spirit is present as your Helper to guide your discussion. Please do not let this become some kind of ritual prayer. Remember, it is an actual invitation.

To Begin Your Discussion:

Read the following introduction out loud to the group:

The world in Jesus' day was not wealthy in the same way we understand it today. But its many beauties and its abundance still attracted the eye and produced envy, just like it has all through history. How were the followers of Jesus supposed to deal with the realities of living in a physical world?

Discuss the Following Questions One at a Time.

Read each question out loud and listen to what each person is saying. Ask questions to clarify and develop ideas together as a group. Help each other stay on topic with the reminder, "What does this have to do with the question we are discussing?"

1. What was the economic world like for the Jews at the time of Jesus and His audience in particular? Remember they lived under Roman occupation, and money always tends to flow towards the center of power.

2. Why do you think He chose these three economic topics in particular?

3. Does Jesus seem more concerned about the stuff we pursue or rather the effect of this pursuit on us? How does Jesus compare and contrast the realities of living in a material world with life in a heavenly Kingdom?

4. What might concern Jesus about the materialism of our culture today?

Note some of the ideas that strike you as especially meaningful:

Before you leave, share one or two of these ideas with the group. Read back important highlights from the previous week and add ideas from the current discussion. It is essential that you take a few minutes to do this before you break up the meeting. Continue circulating the notes. Use your text group or other social media tools to raise additional questions for further discussion but try not to get too far off the main subject. Don't forget that keeping a journal for yourself is also helpful.

Close with a prayer of thanksgiving and expectation that God will continue to show you more.

Take a little time this evening to read the following for further personal reflection:

Sit comfortably, close your eyes, with no phone, no Bible, and no notepad. This is a time for you to just be in the presence of Jesus. Always begin by inviting the Holy Spirit to speak. Let thoughts go past you as you use this as sacred time with God. This is spiritual listening, and quiet is the sound of Jesus connecting with your soul, not your conscious mind. Remember that your subconscious mind is working, and your spirit is responding whether you are conscious of it or not.

Don't forget to be patient and cut yourself some slack. If there is a lot of noise in your head, try using your "sacred word" or phrase of a favorite song to call yourself back from the chaos!

Week 5 Headline:

The Path to Social Justice

I am really tired of trying to figure out political correctness. It seems to trivialize the very real issues that underly the injustices that so many face. Jesus saw the same problems in His day. He taught that the system of social justice, which the Jewish people depended on, simply didn't work because of the intrinsic self-centered bias of everyone seeking justice. The success of the new heavenly realm would require a new approach based on personal spiritual discernment rather than an external judgment system.

Jesus teaches this new approach in five key principles for daily living in a sinful and self-centered world. First, He taught that we should always begin by looking at ourselves as the problem when something seems unfair. Second, we should always look to our heavenly Father when there is need. We must remember His love and provision are equally available for all, and we need only ask when there is need. Third, He challenges us to remember the Kingdom of Heaven provides refuge for all who seek it. But this requires keeping a careful watch at the gate for bad actors who would enter to do harm. Fourth, we must remember that bad behavior is more telling than nice words. Sincerity is not enough to ensure trustworthiness. We must weigh what people do, not just what they say.

It seems to me that the tragic failure of many churches today is not hypocrisy or judgmentalism. Though we can rightly be accused of it, the problem goes far deeper. I think we live in a church culture that is quick to point the finger at the failure of others rather than take responsibility for the issues of social injustice. I understand it is difficult to do. There are many risks. But do we really need a minefield of doctrinal issues and social hoops through which people must pass to get what they need? By its bad example, our religious culture often seems to teach that we must stand up for our individual rights rather than embrace all who seek help. I think you would agree that we desperately need those who live by the Wisdom of Jesus in the new heavenly Kingdom, and we need churches that encourage it.

Before You Meet:

Spend some time familiarizing yourself with the teaching you will be investigating. Read Matthew 7:1-27. It's a shorter read this week, so consider taking some extra time to examine it a little more closely.

To Begin Your Meeting:

Read this week's headline and then Matthew 7:1-27 out loud. Invite Jesus to join you and answer some questions. Thankfully acknowledge that His Spirit is present as your Helper to guide your discussion. Please do not let this become some kind of ritual prayer. Remember, it is an actual invitation.

To Begin Your Discussion:

Read the following introduction out loud to the group:

Jesus concludes His sermon with a look at social life. It makes sense that Jesus would want to guide His followers with a new strategy for daily living. After all, He was inviting them to a new spiritual Kingdom on earth. But why does He focus on the issue of social justice? It was just as divisive then as it is now. How does Jesus avert a debate that damages His ministry?

Discuss the Following Questions One at a Time.

Read each question out loud and listen to what each person is saying. Ask questions to clarify and develop ideas together as a group. Help each other stay on topic with the reminder, "What does this have to do with the question we are discussing?"

1. How did the Jewish community view the issues of social justice? Remember, God had given the twelve brothers of Israel a code (the Torah), which was supposed to help their families (tribes) live together successfully as a society and produce what they called *shalom* (well-being). But they lived in a time when the tribal system had completely disintegrated.

2. Jesus addresses five key issues in Matthew 7 that put responsibility for social justice back on the individual instead of on a system of religious or political rules. Why do you think Jesus chose these five particular topics? To help you, read each of the following segments one at a time as a specific topic: Matthew 7:1-6, 7:7-12, 7:13-14, 7:15-20, and 7:21-27.

3. How does Jesus compare and contrast the realities of social injustices with life in His heavenly Kingdom?

4. How do we address this today in our culture of tolerance and non-judgmentalism?

Note some of the ideas that strike you as especially meaningful.

Before you leave, share one or two of these ideas with the group. Read back important highlights from the previous week and add ideas from the current discussion. It is essential that you take a few minutes to do this before you break up the meeting. Continue circulating the notes. Use your text group or other social media tools to raise additional questions for further discussion but try not to get too far off the main subject. Don't forget that keeping a journal for yourself is also helpful.

Close with a prayer of thanksgiving and expectation that God will continue to show you more.

Within a day or two of your discussion, take at least one 15-minute time-out to allow Jesus to have easy access to your heart.

Sit comfortably, close your eyes, with no phone, no Bible, and no notepad. This is a time for you to just be in the presence of Jesus. Always begin by inviting the Holy Spirit to speak. Let thoughts go past you as you use this as sacred time with God. This is spiritual listening, and quiet is the sound of Jesus connecting with your soul, not your conscious mind. Remember that your subconscious mind is working, and your spirit is responding whether you are conscious of it or not.

Don't forget to be patient and cut yourself some slack. If there is a lot of noise in your head, try using your "sacred word" or the phrase of a special song to call yourself back from the chaos!

Digging Deeper Into The Central Messages Of Jesus' Teaching

Key question:

How did Jesus' message about the Kingdom of God reveal a path of restoration for humanity? How does this change everything for humanity?

Discuss this statement:

The radical teaching of Jesus upends the view that thoughts and actions are all that matters. Jesus teaches that the human heart—who and what we love— is at the center of the issues we face as followers of Jesus in a fallen world.

To prepare for your next feature story:

Consider the following questions: The key encounters and teachings of Jesus work together to give us a picture of Jesus and what He came to do on earth as the Messiah. But how are we to respond to these things? HOW can we embrace these truths despite the limitations and sufferings of our mortal existence?

Feature Story #3:
An Invisible Kingdom Gives Hope to Humanity

How the reality of a new spiritual domain changes everything.

In Part 1 we learned that the events in Jesus' life marked a turning point for humanity and a major shift in the spiritual realm. So far in Part 2 we have discovered that Jesus Himself reveals the path to the restoration of human dignity, spirituality, freedom, and justice. Feature Story 3 is a continuation from Feature Story 2. Jesus' life was far more than just a series of well-choreographed prophetic events and a sermon or two. We need to find out more about what was going on behind the scenes! How did Jesus interact with his inner circle? Why *did* the life of Jesus actually change the world?

Obviously, many things were quite different at the time of Jesus. Back then, there were no festive religious holidays, no megachurch meetings, no Christian concert events, and no bumper sticker slogans about loving others. Back then, a small group of renegade Jews spread a story that awoke a passion for a way of life the world had never seen. Followers of Jesus were living as if the Creator God was living in them and through them! It was a story unique to the early followers of Jesus.

You could argue that the people who believed this story were just religious zealots—poorly educated and uncivilized. You might think they would believe such things since, after all, science and technology as we know it did not exist. Democracy and the Internet had not even been invented yet. There was no such thing as the English language or social media. So what were the key factors in producing this radical social movement? That's what you and your team of investigators need to find out in this next feature story: *An Invisible Kingdom Gives Hope to Humanity*!

We will continue with the Gospel of Matthew as our primary source for this story. As you learned in Feature Story #2, the Gospel of Matthew is uniquely organized. It appears to be an orientation guide for those who wanted to follow Jesus—the One whom Matthew believed was the newly enthroned King of the world. But this Gospel offers so much more. It contains key teachings that seem designed to guide novice followers of Jesus the Rabbi to a mature relationship with Jesus the King.

As you begin your next series of discussions, pay particular attention to how Matthew shows Jesus communicating cross-culturally and cross-generationally. Sometimes, He is speaking to large crowds and sometime to His inner circle. Clearly, Matthew was aware that people of all sorts needed help. He himself was an outsider at one time (remember Matthew was once the hated tax collector). I have found that Matthew's Gospel is an ideal source to expose the plan behind what Jesus accomplished.

The scope of this Feature Story is a little broader than your previous projects. This one will require a bit more Bible reading. But don't be discouraged. Each question contains specific references from the longer readings to help you focus on the main thought. A bit of study is involved, but don't forget: the main point is to enjoy your discussions!

Week 6 Headline:

A New Way to See the World

Sometimes I try to imagine myself as one of those early followers of Jesus. There I am uprooted from my simple life to a life of watching and learning from a man who is upending the world as I know it. I am sure it was different being there, hearing and seeing the events. But no matter, I am also confident I would not have been ready for my first assignment. I am not sure I would have even expected it! But Jesus seems to think His disciples have been watching long enough. He is ready to send them out.

Jesus has given them a new way to see the world through the eyes of faith, and now, He expects them to exercise their faith by delivering a simple message. The message? The Kingdom of Heaven has come. By faith, Jesus wants the disciples to align themselves with the sacrificial journey He is making to establish His Kingdom. But they each need to work out how.

The disciples know that physical harm is not to be feared but expected, and that spiritual victory is to be embraced in the already established authority of Jesus. And they seem to understand that they are to freely share what they freely received (The Kingdom), giving up their lives for the Life they can never really lose in Jesus. Their first mission without Jesus physically present proves to be an invaluable lesson about how to do life without Jesus physically at their side! There are many failures along the way as the disciples start engaging the fallen world using a new faith, not their old religious habits.

I remember this same challenge as my wife and I started out forty years ago planting and developing churches. Our journey following Jesus eventually led to full-time international missions, all the while living on the edge between our faith and our fear. It is well to consider the wise words of Jim Elliot, a missionary who gave his life to Jesus: "He is no fool who gives what he cannot keep, to gain what he cannot lose." He died doing so. Faith that Jesus is actively working to expand His Kingdom is the one thing that everyone who follows Jesus needs to be able to navigate the fallen world. Why not take the same challenge Jesus gave His first disciples!

Before You Meet:

Spend some time familiarizing yourself with the teaching you will be investigating. Read Matthew 8–10. Note the limited variety of miracles.

To Begin Your Meeting:

Read this week's headline and then Matthew 9:35–11:1 out loud. Invite Jesus to join you and answer some questions. Thankfully acknowledge that His Spirit is present as your Helper to guide your discussion. Please do not let this become some kind of ritual prayer. Remember, it is an actual invitation.

To Begin Your Discussion:

Read the following introduction out loud to the group:

Matthew chooses specific miracles designed to show us the importance and nature of *faith* as the connection to God's long-promised plan for advancing His new Kingdom on earth. We will look at nine examples given by Matthew, but I am sure many more were performed to signal the coming of God's Kingdom.

Jesus sends out His inner circle with a simple message announcing this new Kingdom, but He asks them to do so in a very specific way and to a very specific group of people. How does Jesus use these early experiences to help His disciples see the coming changes?

Discuss the Following Questions One at a Time.

Read each question out loud and listen to what each person is saying. Ask questions to clarify and develop ideas together as a group. Help each other stay on topic with the reminder, "What does this have to do with the question we are discussing?"

1. What do the stories and teaching about faith reveal about the coming of the promised Kingdom? How did this prepare the disciples for their first assignment?

2. What did Jesus expect of His disciples in this first major assignment? Remember that John the Baptist was already in prison and that Jesus had come to give His own people one last chance to be the nation God intended.

3. Why does Jesus encourage His disciples that the "harvest is plentiful" (Matthew 9:37) and at the same time remind them that they will often be rejected (Matthew 10:22-23)?

4. How can we prepare ourselves to follow in the footsteps of the disciples as we navigate our own spiritual journey?

Note some of the ideas that strike you as especially meaningful:

Before you leave, share one or two of these ideas with the group. Read back important highlights from the previous week and add ideas from the current discussion. It is essential that you take a few minutes to do this before you break up the meeting. Continue circulating the notes. Use your text group or other social media tools to raise additional questions for further discussion but try not to get too far off the main subject. Don't forget that keeping a journal for yourself is also helpful.

Close with a prayer of thanksgiving and expectation that God will continue to show you more.

Within a day or two of your discussion, take at least one 15-minute time-out to allow Jesus to have easy access to your heart.

Sit comfortably, close your eyes, with no phone, no Bible, and no notepad. This is a time for you to just be in the presence of Jesus. Always begin by inviting the Holy Spirit to speak. Let thoughts go past you as you use this as sacred time with God. This is spiritual listening, and quiet is the sound of Jesus connecting with your soul, not your conscious mind. Remember that your subconscious mind is working, and your spirit is responding whether you are conscious of it or not.

Don't forget to be patient and cut yourself some slack. If there is a lot of noise in your head, try using your "sacred word" or phrase from a favorite song to call yourself back from the chaos!

Week 7 Headline:

The New Spiritual Domain of Jesus Is Not Everyone's Cup of Tea

I wish it were easy to see the reality of a spiritual domain on earth. It seems like it should be obvious, given how we often face the unexplainable. But it's not. In fact, humanity has always struggled to understand the reality of our spirituality. It was no different in Jesus' day. Matthew carefully weaves together a series of eight parables to explain the nature of the spiritual domain (including an angelic army) to those who lived in a religious world. The parables he shares help us see the complexity surrounding the launch of God's Kingdom in a fallen world, which does not acknowledge its good Creator. The response to the Good News is disappointingly varied despite the simplicity of the message.

To the crowds, Jesus offers a simple invitation to receive His message. Like a Sower, Jesus expects a good harvest produced by hearts ready to receive His spiritual message. He knows that bad seed is also being sown by other sowers, but this is not His concern because every single good seed has the potential to produce enormous benefit, regardless of the bad. And like leaven, the message of the Kingdom will inconspicuously permeate every bit of the harvest the Sower will eventually reap.

To His inner circle, Jesus poses a simple but paradoxical challenge—share My message that has been intentionally hidden. Jesus uses two more parables to show how the new spiritual domain had to remain partially veiled until its full value could be revealed. By hiding it in plain sight, those who saw its value would be willing to pay the price for it. It was not up to the disciples to make it more attractive.

And one last problem: As the Kingdom was being established, the disciples would have little control over who would join them. They would need to trust that just like the harvest is sorted out, their "catch" would be sorted out as well. Their only job was to consistently display the Kingdom's treasures, both old and new, for the world to see. They could not control how people would respond, but they could present the opportunity and then leave the rest to God.

It's this last problem that challenges me the most. I'm a surgeon living in a messy world full of unpredictable responses. It's not my preferred way to work! But these stories help me mentally and spiritually prepare for a life of uncertainty that goes with following Jesus. I can be confident that the unstoppable Kingdom will prevail no matter what.

Before You Meet:

Spend some time familiarizing yourself with the teaching you will be investigating. Read Matthew 11–13. Pay particular attention to the various audiences and responses.

To Begin Your Meeting:

Read this week's headline and then Matthew 13:1-52 out loud. Invite Jesus to join you and answer some questions. Thankfully acknowledge that His Spirit is present as your Helper to guide your discussion. Please do not let this become some kind of ritual prayer. Remember, it is an actual invitation.

To Begin Your Discussion:

Read the following introduction out loud to the group:

Matthew makes it clear in Chapters 11 and 12 that there was a wide spectrum of responses to Jesus' message: Some believe, some doubt, and some even defiantly reject what Jesus says. The disciples face growing hostility and angry skepticism. As a result, Jesus makes a change in His teaching strategy. Instead of pointed sermons, Jesus pivots to using enigmatic parables, which even His disciples sometimes do not understand. Why does Jesus seemingly try to make it more difficult to understand His message? Why not just lay out the facts if so many are already having trouble understanding what He is teaching?

Discuss the Following Questions One at a Time.

Read each question out loud and listen to what each person is saying. Ask questions to clarify and develop ideas together as a group. Help each other stay on topic with the reminder, "What does this have to do with the question we are discussing?"

1. How does Jesus use a series of agricultural parables like a sort of coded message to attract genuine followers? To help, read Matthew 13:1-9 and 24-33 out loud and discuss how these four parables build on each other.

2. How could this new strategy possibly help His cause? To help, read Matthew 13:10-17 and 34-35 out loud and discuss.

3. Matthew then recaps four additional parables told to the inner circle (Matthew 13:36-52). How do these parables build on each other to paint a realistic picture of what the disciples can expect going forward?

4. How do these parables make it clear that Jesus was *not* promoting a religious movement? Remember that these were as common in Jesus' day as they are today.

Note some of the ideas that strike you as especially meaningful.

Before you leave, share one or two of these ideas with the group. Read back important highlights from the previous week and add ideas from the current discussion. It is essential that you take a few minutes to do this before you break up the meeting. Continue circulating the notes. Use your text group or other social media tools to raise additional questions for further discussion but try not to get too far off the main subject. Don't forget that keeping a journal for yourself is also helpful.

Close with a prayer of thanksgiving and expectation that God will continue to show you more.

Within a day or two of your discussion, take at least one 15-minute time-out to allow Jesus to have easy access to your heart.

Sit comfortably, close your eyes, with no phone, no Bible, and no notepad. This is a time for you to just be in the presence of Jesus. Always begin by inviting the Holy Spirit to speak. Let thoughts go past you as you use this as sacred time with God. This is spiritual listening, and quiet is the sound of Jesus connecting with your soul, not your conscious mind. Remember that your subconscious mind is working, and your spirit is responding whether you are conscious of it or not.

Don't forget to be patient and cut yourself some slack. If there is a lot of noise in your head, try using your "sacred word" or phrase from a favorite song to call yourself back from the chaos!

Week 8 Headline:

Politics and Religion Threaten the New Spiritual Movement of Jesus

It seems to me that it's time for a review. We've covered a lot of ground and sometimes it's useful to stop and reflect a bit. In the Sermon on the Mount (Matthew 5–7), Jesus lays a foundation for His new heavenly domain on earth. He reveals the path designed by His Father to bring blessing, significance, reward, and spiritual discernment in the New Covenant Kingdom.

Jesus instructs His disciples in the fundamentals of faith and presents them with their primary message and mandate for this new Kingdom (Matthew 8–9). They are to freely give what they have freely received from Jesus. He is clear that the life they give up produces a new Life they cannot lose as citizens of the eternal Kingdom on earth (Matthew 10).

Given the unpredictable responses of those presented with this message, Jesus issues a bold challenge to invest themselves fully in their role as laborers. Jesus is confident that, despite the opposition, His Kingdom is an unstoppable spiritual reality (Matthew 11-13).

That brings us to this week. In Matthew 14–16, Matthew makes it clear that the opposition is also a clear and present danger. He presents the physical hardship of a spiritual Life that is submitted to Jesus. Matthew is brutally honest about the completely senseless death of John the Baptist, who was killed at the whim of a politician's wife and teenage daughter, for stating his moral convictions.

I don't know about you, but it makes me cringe to think life can be so unfair. John dies an ignoble and unjust death. It makes me wonder what I would do. These few verses we investigated today in Matthew 16 present us with the most important question any of us will ever answer: Does life end with death or does it begin? Is it actually possible for "self" to die in the new spiritual realm of Jesus? I believe it is, but it's a painful process!

Before You Meet:

Spend some time familiarizing yourself with the teaching you will be investigating. Read Matthew 14–16. Once again, welcome to a fairly long section of reading, but note how the intensity is building and that Jesus is becoming more focused on the end He knows is coming.

To Begin Your Meeting:

Read this week's headline and then Matthew 16:24-28 out loud. Invite Jesus to join you and answer some questions. Thankfully acknowledge that His Spirit is present as your Helper to guide your discussion. Please do not let this become some kind of ritual prayer. Remember, it is an actual invitation.

To Begin Your Discussion:

Read the following introduction out loud to the group:

Life is getting more intense for the disciples. John the Baptist, the founder of the movement, is unjustly beheaded by Herod, a corrupt Roman political ruler of Israel. This event seems to drag the whole political system into a paranoid fit that something big and disruptive is stirring. In fact, Herod thinks that Jesus, the new leader of the movement, is actually the ghost of John.

Jesus begins to operate more from the shadows as He continues to perform the miracles that signify the beginning of a new Kingdom. The Pharisees are becoming more vocal about their disapproval as Jesus becomes more aggressive with His miracles. He is disturbing the equilibrium with Rome, which they had worked so hard to achieve. Here lies the perfect opportunity for Jesus to break the news to His inner circle about what would be required of them. But they would not like what they hear.

Discuss the Following Questions One at a Time.

Read each question out loud and listen to what each person is saying. Ask questions to clarify and develop ideas together as a group. Help each other stay on topic with the reminder, "What does this have to do with the question we are discussing?"

1. Based on what we have studied so far, if someone asked you what is the "good news" Jesus announced, what would you say? What do you think Matthew would say?

2. What three things does Jesus ask of His followers? You might want to read Matthew 16:24-28 out loud again. How does this relate to what we have learned about the new Kingdom?

3. How does Jesus serve as an example of the same faith He requires of us?

4. Why do we assume that faith costs us nothing? What are some ways Jesus might ask you to pay the price of faith?

Note some of the ideas that strike you as especially meaningful:

Before you leave, share one or two of these ideas with the group. Read back important highlights from the previous week and add ideas from the current discussion. It is essential that you take a few minutes to do this before you break up the meeting. Continue circulating the notes. Use your text group or other social media tools to raise additional questions for further discussion but try not to get too far off the main subject. Don't forget that keeping a journal for yourself is also helpful.

Close with a prayer of thanksgiving and expectation that God will continue to show you more.

Within a day or two of your discussion, take at least one 15-minute time-out to allow Jesus to have easy access to your heart.

Sit comfortably, close your eyes, with no phone, no Bible, and no notepad. This is a time for you to just be in the presence of Jesus. Always begin by inviting the Holy Spirit to speak. Let thoughts go past you as you use this as sacred time with God. This is spiritual listening, and quiet is the sound of Jesus connecting with your soul, not your conscious mind. Remember that your subconscious mind is working, and your spirit is responding whether you are conscious of it or not.

Don't forget to be patient and cut yourself some slack. If there is a lot of noise in your head, try using your "sacred word" or phrase from a favorite song to call yourself back from the chaos!

Week 9 Headline:

A Bold, New Style Of Leadership Turns The New Spiritual Movement On Its Head

I have never been one to seek recognition. Sometimes it comes anyway, and then it's a bit of a surprise to me. In my view, the pursuit of greatness only adds an extra burden to the challenges of getting the job done well. Why make it harder trying to look good? The disciples almost frantically question who would be greatest in the coming Kingdom while wondering if that Kingdom would even come. Jesus confronts their misguided thinking by explaining what greatness actually looks like in His Kingdom. Jesus likens the appearance of greatness to that of a child with no legal standing, no political power, and seemingly no influence. These "children" (literally and metaphorically) are precisely those whom Jesus is seeking to lead His new domain. There is much to do, and Jesus asks the disciples to humbly forgo their own grandiose agendas to align themselves with His ministry.

Matthew then lays out in detail the attitudes and commitment it would take to be leaders in Jesus' ministry of restoration. First, it would require that they forgive more than they had ever forgiven before. Second, a confrontation with the Pharisees over the legitimacy of divorce shows the followers of Jesus that their choice to follow Him should come first but never at the expense of their integrity (see Matthew 19:10-12). Third and perhaps most difficult, following Jesus would necessitate setting aside the desire for status associated with riches (like the rich, young ruler failed to do). Fourth, Matthew uses Jesus' parable of the ungrateful worker to expose the desire to be rewarded as nothing more than ungrateful self-centeredness. He concludes with the challenge to see that the greatness of the Messiah is demonstrated in His humble submission to sacrificial service and death for all, even for His enemies.

It's a lot to ask! There was indeed greatness in the Kingdom, but it would require practicing forgiveness, giving up status, setting priorities with integrity, giving up the right to the reward we think we deserve, and living sacrificially. Along with the disciples, we are all called to this same path. I believe that greatness in the domain of Jesus on earth looks like humility and faithful servanthood. The spiritual domain we cannot physically see shows up in how we act.

I love how this message is so poignantly displayed in the scene where Jesus washes the disciples' feet. Take a minute to read it yourself in John 13:1-17. I hope you agree with me that the significance of servant leadership is worth the price we must pay for it.

Before You Meet:

Spend some time familiarizing yourself with the teaching you will be investigating. Read Matthew 17–20:28. Review your notes from Week 5 in Feature Story #1 regarding the transfiguration event recorded in Matthew 17. Pay special attention to how this section begins and ends with a discussion of who will be the greatest. Note how the stories may contribute to an understanding of greatness.

To Begin Your Meeting:

Read this week's headline and then Matthew 18:1-6 and 20:20-28 out loud. Invite Jesus to join you and answer some questions. Thankfully acknowledge that His Spirit is present as your Helper to guide your discussion. Please do not let this become some kind of ritual prayer. Remember, it is an actual invitation.

To Begin Your Discussion:

Read the following introduction out loud to the group:

The new spiritual movement needed a boost. The rejection at Nazareth, the beheading of John the Baptist, and the increasing hostility from the Jewish religious elite took a toll. There were fewer supportive crowds, and within His own small camp, Peter declares Jesus to be the Messiah, God's Son, but then does not accept His sacrificial journey to the cross.

Then, in Matthew 17, Jesus has a miraculous encounter with the founding prophets of the nation of Israel and with His heavenly Father. But He instructs the few who witness it to keep it a secret! Instead of celebrating this Holy visitation, the disciples are forced to confront the weakness of their faith, even as Jesus warns them about His coming death. Jesus encourages them that their faith would one day move mountains. Then, by miraculously paying their temple tax, He also reminds them that they are sons of a new Kingdom, free from the constraints of their old religious system.

It all seems a bit confusing. Was everything they hoped for slipping away or was there still a chance for greatness?

Discuss the Following Questions One at a Time.

Read each question out loud and listen to what each person is saying. Ask questions to clarify and develop ideas together as a group. Help each other stay on topic with the reminder, "What does this have to do with the question we are discussing?"

1. Why the sudden interest in greatness among the disciples?

2. Did Jesus idolize children? They are mentioned twice in this section of Matthew. How do they help us understand greatness?

3. Matthew puts together a series of stories, teachings, and parables that seem to lay out what would be required of the disciples if they truly wanted to be great in God's Kingdom. How were each of these things countercultural? What is the common denominator?

4. What is the fundamental difference between being a servant-leader and being a leader who serves?

Note some of the ideas that strike you as especially meaningful.

Before you leave, share one or two of these ideas with the group. Read back important highlights from the previous week and add ideas from the current discussion. It is essential that you take a few minutes to do this before you break up the meeting. Continue circulating the notes. Use your text group or other social media tools to raise additional questions for further discussion but try not to get too far off the main subject. Don't forget that keeping a journal for yourself is also helpful.

Close with a prayer of thanksgiving and expectation that God will continue to show you more.

Within a day or two of your discussion, take at least one 15-minute time-out to allow Jesus to have easy access to your heart.

Sit comfortably, close your eyes, with no phone, no Bible, and no notepad. This is a time for you to just be in the presence of Jesus. Always begin by inviting the Holy Spirit to speak. Let thoughts go past you as you use this as sacred time with God. This is spiritual listening, and quiet is the sound of Jesus connecting with your soul not your conscious mind. Remember that your subconscious mind is working, and your spirit is responding whether you are conscious of it or not.

Don't forget to be patient and cut yourself some slack. If there is a lot of noise in your head, try using your "sacred word" or phrase from a favorite song to call yourself back from the chaos!

Week 10 Headline:

Jesus Asserts His Authority Despite Rising Discontent

One of the most important things in my life has been figuring out who I am following and why. I wanted to know because I believe it is naïve to think I am not following somebody. We all do! Jesus is well aware that He has asked for complete obedience from His followers. In fact, He is about to show them what obedience looks like as He submits Himself to an unjust death on a Roman cross. But under whose authority does Jesus act? What right has He to ask for obedience?

Jesus makes it clear that His Father is the source of His authority. His sovereign Father has delegated authority to Him. He can give the new Kingdom to, or take it from, whomever He wishes. When Jesus' authority as the rightful heir to His Father's Kingdom is questioned by those seeking power for themselves, Jesus uses a series of parables to explain what legitimate, God-given authority should look like. He portrays genuine authority like a caring father who is willing to wait for his disrespectful son to do the right thing or a gracious landowner providing justice for his son who is viciously attacked. Jesus describes authentic royal power by telling the story of a loving King who organizes a beautiful wedding for his son and then responds in anger to his disinterested and ungrateful subjects.

Jesus asserts that His divinely delegated authority is superior to Caesar's illegitimate claim to divine power by pointing out that Caeser is a mere head on a coin. And with His first royal decree, Jesus supersedes even the divine Mosaic Law with the Two Great Commandments to love God and love our neighbor as ourselves. Only Jesus could declare the law fulfilled by these two great commandments.

Jesus goes head-to-head with the religious elite (Pharisees, Scribes, and Sadducees) as well as the political elite (Herodians and lawyers). He exposes how they usurp power without any real authority as proven by their hypocrisy, their spiritual blindness, and their guilty association with murderers, liars, and thieves.

Jesus gives His final teaching to the disciples on the Mount of Olives. This was a site of enormous prophetic significance for the coming of the new Kingdom (see Zechariah 14:1-9). Here Jesus describes how the world will look in their generation as the new Kingdom comes. At first, Jesus' ascent to the throne will only produce hardship and suffering for His followers. Many will fall away, primarily because of those who falsely and violently assert their authority as leaders of this world. Jesus explains that they must prepare, like faithful and wise servants caring for the master's household, and like those who prepare wisely for the long feasting of a wedding celebration. As bad as things will get, they can and will enjoy "the wedding." (I think this is a picture of heaven and earth joining together.) He encourages them by saying that they are not responsible for those who do not respond, and that they will be rewarded if they faithfully invest what He has given them.

As a final encouragement to all of us, Jesus describes how the story will play out at some unknown point in the future. His authority over heaven and earth will one day be fully and visibly restored in all its glory. There is no stopping the final enthronement of Jesus. The Father will hand the Kingdom over to His Son and, along with it, His right to share His inheritance with whomever He wishes.

In the end, there will be no interference in the transfer of His inheritance to all those who have come in faith to the Kingdom. This is a right He has "prepared for them from the foundation of the world." Jesus will stop at nothing to finish what He has started, and He will faithfully execute justice by sharing His authority with those who desire the Kingdom. But He will eliminate those who want no part of it.

I believe that Jesus, who Himself is fully God, had the power and right to act independently. But He chose to act under the authority of His Father. No matter how much power I am given to lead and no matter what my rights may be, I am always asked to follow the model of Jesus who gave up His rights and His power in the most mysterious, most incredible display of submission ever. Take a minute to read and reflect on Philippians 2:1-11. It's one of my favorite pieces of Paul's writing.

Before You Meet:

Spend some time familiarizing yourself with the teaching you will be investigating by skimming through the section titles of Matthew 21–25. This is a complex and somewhat lengthy reading, but it provides critical information about how the path to the restoration of humanity is secured by Jesus. It is well worth a detailed read if you have time to go for the full background.

In addition, if you have time and interest, the prophetic language used by Matthew in this section shows up in Psalm 118 (the One who comes in the name of the Lord), Daniel 9–12 (the desolation of Jerusalem), and Zechariah 14:1-9 (the coming of the Day of the Lord to restore His authority over all creation).

To Begin Your Meeting:

Read this week's headline and then Matthew 21:23-27, 43-46 out loud. Invite Jesus to join you and answer some questions. Thankfully acknowledge that His Spirit is present as your Helper to guide your discussion. Please do not let this become some kind of ritual prayer. Remember, it is an actual invitation.

To Begin Your Discussion:

Read the following introduction out loud to the group:

The time for teaching is nearly over. Matthew pulls back the curtain to let us see Jesus' royal authority as He heals blindness, takes back His house (the temple), and directly commands creation. Clearly, Jesus has had this authority all along but now is asserting it more directly, and not at all like the authority of those who live for the world.

This predictably results in more intimidation and planning for His execution. A triumphal entry into Jerusalem is quickly followed by death threats. Jesus shows the disciples the distinction between legitimate and illegitimate authority in a series of confrontations, parables, and stories. The disciples will soon be facing the greatest test of their loyalty and commitment to the mission of Jesus. On whose side will they stand?

Discuss the Following Questions One at a Time.

Read each question out loud and listen to what each person is saying. Ask questions to clarify and develop ideas together as a group. Help each other stay on topic with the reminder, "What does this have to do with the question we are discussing?"

1. How does Jesus begin asserting His royal authority in Chapters 21–22?

2. Why does Jesus bother to confront the illegitimate authority of the Pharisees and the politicians (see Matthew 23:1-26)?

3. What is so significant about the Mount of Olives as the setting for where Jesus shares about the coming Kingdom (see Zechariah 14:1-9)?

4. What does Jesus' ascent to the throne look like in our time and when the end finally comes? What should be our response?

Note some of the ideas that strike you as especially meaningful.

Before you leave, share one or two of these ideas with the group. Read back important highlights from the previous week and add ideas from the current discussion. It is essential that you take a few minutes to do this before you break up the meeting. Continue circulating the notes. Use your text group or other social media tools to raise additional questions for further discussion but try not to get too far off the main subject. Don't forget that keeping a journal for yourself is also helpful.

Close with a prayer of thanksgiving and expectation that God will continue to show you more.

Within a day or two of your discussion, take at least one 15-minute time-out to allow Jesus to have easy access to your heart.

Sit comfortably, close your eyes, with no phone, no Bible, and no notepad. This is a time for you to just be in the presence of Jesus. Always begin by inviting the Holy Spirit to speak. Let thoughts go past you as you use this as sacred time with God. This is spiritual listening, and quiet is the sound of Jesus connecting with your soul, not your conscious mind. Remember that your subconscious mind is working, and your spirit is responding whether you are conscious of it or not.

Don't forget to be patient and cut yourself some slack. If there is a lot of noise in your head, try using your "sacred word" or phrase from a favorite song to call yourself back from the chaos!

Week 11 Headline:

Jesus Declares Victory for His New Domain

I am sure you would agree that this is a climactic ending to the long struggle of Jesus to capture the hearts of His people and His followers. I have often read it with a sort of finality. But it's actually a bit of a cliffhanger. Matthew calls out to us—using Jesus' final words to His closest followers—as a challenge to us that it's time to step up. Some still doubted, even though they saw the resurrected Jesus with an immortal body. But with one final command, Jesus asks them all to go about life in the light of something bigger than the physical world.

Just three years before, Jesus had invited the first disciples to look beyond being fishermen to living a life as "fishers of men." Now they are being challenged to practice the messy, unpredictable, and often disappointing reality of that life as taught and modeled by Jesus. Before Jesus came into their lives, the disciples frequently recited the Shema ("Hear, O Israel, the Lord your God is One"). Now they are instructed to identify and operate under the name of the Father, the Son, and the Holy Spirit as the fullness of the One into whom they are literally "baptized."

I think Matthew leaves the ending as a tantalizing challenge to us all. It is a climactic victory, yes. And the fulfillment of the loving promise of God to use His Life as the source for the restoration of His creation had begun (See John 3:16-17). But would the followers of Jesus now act in faith in this new Kingdom on earth with the authority given to them by the immortal Jesus, seated on His heavenly throne? What would *we* do with this new reality? You have now finished your report on this fantastic Feature Story about "An Invisible Kingdom Giving Hope to Humanity." Now we all must decide what to do with this hope!

Before You Meet:

Spend some time familiarizing yourself with the teaching you will be investigating. Read Matthew 26–28. To fill in a bit more of the story, I would suggest you also review Acts 1:1-11 and Luke 24:36-53.

To Begin Your Meeting:

Read this week's headline and then Matthew 28:16-20 out loud. Invite Jesus to join you and answer some questions. Thankfully acknowledge that His Spirit is present as your Helper to guide your discussion. Please do not let this become some kind of ritual prayer. Remember, it is an actual invitation.

To Begin Your Discussion:

Read the following introduction out loud to the group:

The events that unfold in the last few chapters of Matthew tell the story of love and sacrifice. For most of us, these are the Bible stories we know best, and rightly so. They are the stories of the suffering Messiah who is finally inaugurated as the divine resurrected King. The curse on humanity is broken, the power of death defeated, and the resurrection power of Jesus is finally released to the world. It is in these stories that we truly see the importance of embracing Jesus. Is He or isn't He the only hope for restoration of humanity?

Discuss the Following Questions One at a Time.

Read each question out loud and listen to what each person is saying. Ask questions to clarify and develop ideas together as a group. Help each other stay on topic with the reminder, "What does this have to do with the question we are discussing?"

1. How do the series of events in Matthew 26–28 (Jesus' betrayal; death; and resurrection with an immortal body) prove that His claim to the Messianic throne is real and legitimate?

2. What is significant about the Mount of Olives as the site of the final challenge from Jesus?

3. Was this the end of His mission on earth or just the beginning?

4. Where did Jesus go, and how is it that Jesus can be with us always?

Note some of the ideas that strike you as especially meaningful:

Before you leave, share one or two of these ideas with the group. Read back important highlights from the previous week and add ideas from the current discussion. It is essential that you take a few minutes to do this before you break up the meeting. Continue circulating the notes. Use your text group or other social media tools to raise additional questions for further discussion but try not to get too far off the main subject. Don't forget that keeping a journal for yourself is also helpful.

Close with a prayer of thanksgiving and expectation that God will continue to show you more.

Within a day or two of your discussion, take at least one 15-minute time-out to allow Jesus to have easy access to your heart.

Sit comfortably, close your eyes, with no phone, no Bible, and no notepad. This is a time for you to just be in the presence of Jesus. Always begin by inviting the Holy Spirit to speak. Let thoughts go past you as you use this as sacred time with God. This is spiritual listening, and quiet is the sound of Jesus connecting with your soul, not your conscious mind. Remember that your subconscious mind is working, and your spirit is responding whether you are conscious of it or not.

Don't forget to be patient and cut yourself some slack. If there is a lot of noise in your head, try using your "sacred word" or phrase from a favorite song to call yourself back from the chaos!

Digging deeper into the story of an invisible Kingdom that gives us hope.

Key question:

How does the life of Jesus reveal a path of restoration for humanity? How does this give us hope today?

Discuss this statement:

The sacrificial life of Jesus supports the view that our condition as human beings is neither hopeless nor helpless. He proves that there is a path to restoration. He calls us to participate with Him in the greatest redemptive story of all creation.

To prepare for the next part of this series.

Consider the following questions: Since Jesus is a human being like me, can I really trust that He will not disappoint me?

Is faith really enough to become part of His redemptive story? Who or what is really behind the Life that is promised?

Part 3

What was Jesus really like?

Feature Story #4:
The Man Behind the Mystery of a New Life

How Jesus helps us reach new potential as human beings.

In Part 3 in our series, *The Importance of Embracing Jesus,* we begin to uncover the nature and character of Jesus Himself. What was He really like? In this fourth Feature Story, I would like you to begin investigating the person behind the events and teachings we have explored so far. You may recall our first three Feature Stories focused on the events and teachings of Jesus. We learned how Jesus provided a new starting point for humanity, a path to restoration, and a new hope for the future. Now we must look more closely at the man who promised to make it all possible.

This investigation will be based in the Gospel of John. The author (traditionally assumed to be the disciple John) does a good job of capturing the pathos of life in the nation of Israel, originally founded by God to be the hope of the world—a nation which finds itself divided and enslaved in their own land. John's writing confronts his kindred with their opportunity for Life in Jesus, literally standing right in front of their eyes. From John's point of view, Jesus more than adequately proved who He was, but the system He grew up with just couldn't or wouldn't accept it. It was a tragic loss for the nation of Israel but would be a major gain for the world (including a faithful remnant of Israel) that was about to be given access to Life through the blessing of God through faith in Jesus as a fulfillment of the promise to Abraham.

As an investigative reporter, your job is to explore the unique set of stories about Jesus in the Gospel of John. Find out what it was about Him that ignited a spiritual movement in a dead religious nation. Through John's eyes you will immerse yourself in the culture of a faithful remnant of Jews who came to see Jesus as the Source of Life and who carried on His mission to the world. Your assignment is to uncover as much as you can about the person of Jesus and why He is relevant to us today.

I believe the Gospel of John is the perfect source to help you understand Jesus as a person and as a leader. John was an accomplished tradesman who became one of the first followers of Jesus. He was there at the beginning of the revival movement originally led by John the Baptist. When Jesus took over as the leader, John the Apostle became one of His closest friends (along with his brother James and one of his business competitors Peter). The stories of John are told with the heart of this close relationship. At Jesus' crucifixion, John was the one Jesus asked to care for His mother after His death even though she had other sons (John 19:26).

Understanding the Jewish culture in Bible times can present a challenge, but with a little effort, I believe you will enjoy getting into it. The notes and reflections for each headline you explore are designed to help guide you along the way. A few topical Internet searches can fill in other interesting facts. For deeper research, you should consider reading Jewish scholars such as Eli Lizorkin-Eyzenberg's *The Jewish Gospel of John*. But remember the primary goal is for you to enjoy your discussions! That's where the process begins.

Week 1 Headline:

Jesus Arrives on the Scene as the Giver of Life

I wish it were easier to see the great truths of life. Wouldn't it be awesome if someone could just sum it all up in a sentence or two? Or maybe with a Bible verse or two? Unfortunately, truth doesn't work that way. It's more like a story than a proposition. It exists as a solid foundation but also as a flowing river. Nowhere is this more beautifully demonstrated than in the introduction to the Gospel of John. John reminds his readers of some very old stories with some very new twists. Jesus is portrayed as the Creator who filled a new world with the breath of His Spirit, but also as the human leader breathing Life into a radical new spiritual movement. He is represented as the Deliverer of Israel, but also as the founder of a new Israel. This was not easy for His deeply divided Jewish community to accept.

John carefully writes his Gospel to convince his Jewish readers that Jesus' mission was in fulfilment, not replacement, of the promises they had received. He wanted them to understand that the birth of Jesus' new Kingdom actually paralleled the birth of their own. But unlike their failed state, Jesus launched a Kingdom that could not fail—a Kingdom that would finally bring the blessing of God—giving Life to all the nations. John knew that Jesus was the source of that Life!

But John also wants us to see Jesus as the Deliverer. Just as God provided a lamb for Abraham so that Isaac and his heirs could live on to receive and be a blessing (Genesis 22:10-17), God provides a Lamb to deliver His Son's heirs from death so they can inherit the Kingdom. Of course, we know that the Lamb and the Son are one-in-the-same person, Jesus.

The parallels with the deliverance of Israel do not stop there. By offering sacrificial lambs at each home, Israel was protected from an angel of death released on the world during their Egyptian captivity. These lambs protected each Israelite household while all the Egyptian firstborns died. The presence of Jesus as the Lamb given by God begins a new exodus story. The angel of death does not just pass over because of blood painted on a doorpost as in Egypt. In the new Kingdom of God, death itself has no claim whatsoever over any and all who receive God's Deliverer into their lives!

This analogy between Israel and the founding of a new nation continues. I love how John subtly (almost sarcastically) compares the story of Nathanial to the story of Jacob, the father of the twelve tribes. Jacob obtained his father's blessing by deceit and then, when it was finally time to enter the blessing, he wrestled with God over his rights with such intensity that it broke his hip (Genesis 32:24-32)! In fact, this is what the name "Israel" means! The stories of Jacob, the father of the twelve Israelite tribes, show him in stark contrast to Nathaniel, who was a "true Israelite" without guile. Nathaniel responds to the call of Jesus in simple faith. Jesus promised Nathaniel that he would see the portal between heaven and earth opened directly to Him, instead of to an altar like Jacob saw (Genesis 22:10-17). Imagine that! In fact, all the faithful would come to see the face of God revealed in the face of Jesus.

It truly blows me away to think about it. In one chapter John invites us to recall the birth of the universe and the birth of a new nation through Jesus, the Source of Life and our Deliverer from death. Can it get any better than this? Oh, yes it can! Jesus' first demonstration of the glory of the Life He offers is a story of abundance and joy miraculously provided at a wedding feast (John 2:1-12). This is not some story of Life as a solemn burden we bear but as a party we enjoy! It's a foreshadowing of the fullness of Life and the banquet table where we will one day sit with Jesus in the new heavens and new earth!

Before You Meet:

Spend some time familiarizing yourself with the teaching you will be investigating. Read John 1:1–2:12. To help you with the Jewish context, you should also read Genesis 1:1-4, Genesis 22:10-17, Genesis 28:10-17, Genesis 32:24-32, Isaiah 53:1-12, Amos 9:14, and Jeremiah 31:12. Though I've listed quite a few references, it's not that many verses to read, and they also provide a broad and important introduction to John's Gospel.

To Begin Your Meeting:

Read this week's headline and then John 1:1-4 out loud. Invite Jesus to join you and answer some questions. Thankfully acknowledge that His Spirit is present as your Helper to guide your discussion. I will remind you to do this each week, but please do not let it become some kind of ritual prayer. Remember, it is an actual invitation.

To Begin Your Discussion:

Read the following introduction out loud to the group:

In his introduction, John takes us back to the beginning of time to portray Jesus as the voice of God speaking Life into all creation. All Life finds its source in this divine power who, incredibly, has now become an inextinguishable beacon of Light for *all* humanity (not just the children of Israel)!

John brings Jesus into the story he writes after John the Baptist had already launched a wilderness campaign to deliver Israel from its spiritual exile. When Jesus was baptized to symbolically join in this wilderness movement, everything changes. It became very clear that He was the true leader of this movement and the One who would deliver the nation from slavery. He was the Messiah whom God has specifically provided for the task. God said so Himself!

John portrays Jesus as the full revelation of God, not just a representative of the Law of Moses (the Torah). John passionately explains to his kinsmen that Jesus is not just the divine Source of Life; He is also their Deliverer from slavery and death. The Law of Moses offered neither of these things. Jesus embodied Life and revealed it as grace and truth! All who put their trust in Him, all who see Him as He really is and receive Him, are children of God. I understand why this is difficult for us today, but with Jesus right there in front of them, why was it so hard to believe?

Discuss the Following Questions One at a Time.

Read each question out loud and listen to what each person is saying. Don't forget to ask your own questions to clarify and develop ideas together as a group. Help each other stay on topic with the reminder, "What does this have to do with the question we are discussing?"

1. John connects Jesus to the story of creation (compare John 1:1-4 with Genesis 1:1-4). Why do we need to see this connection to understand the full story here?

2. John connects Jesus to a radical spiritual movement started by His cousin in the wilderness. How does this story of Israel's repentance and deliverance from slavery relate to the mission of Jesus? (Compare John 1:19-28 to Joshua 3 and 4, and Deuteronomy 1:1, 2:7, 8:2.)

3. John connects the mission of Jesus with the story of the founding of Israel as a nation. Note in John 1:5-13 the privilege that is now available to all mankind, not just the children of Israel. What are some ways that the mission of Jesus is comparable to the founding of a nation?

4. Who is at the center of this new nation, and what sort of nation will it be? It will be helpful at this point to compare John 1:29-51 with Genesis 28:10-17 and Genesis 32:22-30.

Note some of the ideas that strike you as especially meaningful.

Before you leave, share one or two of these ideas with the group. It is essential that you take a few minutes to do this before you break up the meeting. It may be helpful to circulate the notes electronically so others can contribute. Use your text group or other social media tools to raise additional questions but try not to get too far off the main subject. Don't forget that keeping a journal for yourself may also be helpful.

Close with a prayer of thanksgiving and expectation that God will continue to show you more.

Within a day or two of your discussion, take at least one 15-minute time-out to allow Jesus to have easy access to your heart.

Sit comfortably, close your eyes, with no phone, no Bible, and no notepad. This is a time for you to just be in the presence of Jesus. Always begin by inviting the Holy Spirit to speak. His is a Voice with no words. Let thoughts go past you as you use this as sacred time with God. This is spiritual listening, and quiet is the sound of Jesus connecting with your soul, not your conscious mind. Remember that your subconscious mind is working, and your spirit is responding whether you are conscious of it or not.

If this is your first time trying spiritual "listening," please review Appendix 2 as an orientation. Don't forget to be patient and cut yourself some slack. If there is a lot of noise in your head, try using a single word to reduce the clutter. With time, you may find a "sacred word" that is very personal to you. Some find it helpful to use a phrase from a favorite song. Don't focus on the word—just use it to call yourself back from the chaos!

Week 2 Headline:

Jesus Exposes the Failure of the Religious System to Give Life

I get a little nervous discussing religion with religious people. They tend to have well-rehearsed answers, betraying a bit of discomfort that becomes defensive when challenged with questions about spiritual things. It makes it hard to have an open and honest conversation. You've got to love how Jesus just wades right into the deep end in His Jewish religious culture!

He begins by trying to physically clean up the temple during one of the major religious festivals. The priests who were supposed to guard the holiness of the temple and the honor of His Father had failed in their responsibility. Jesus angrily cleans up the mess He finds. The place dedicated to making the presence of God accessible to all mankind had become a place of business. This is intolerable for Jesus who represented the very presence of His Father and whose body was dedicated to the task of restoring access for all humanity to enjoy.

The real problem is exposed when it becomes clear that the religious leaders had lost sight of Life as God intended. Chief among these leaders is Nicodemus, who forgot that eternal Life must come "from above," born on the wings of the Spirit of God who, like the wind, comes and goes as He pleases. Nicodemus seems only aware of the physical origin of life. Jesus acknowledges that the Source of Life had indeed been born on earth and would be lifted up on earth so that all who believe would have eternal Life.

John gives us the most exciting news, which he himself had finally come to see: this is what the love of God looks like! In these two stories, John gives us a clear look at the passionate love of Jesus for His Father and indeed for the whole world. He boldly proclaims that God sent His one and only Son to earth so that by faith all who believe in Him can enjoy the Life only God can give (John 3:16). But Jesus clarifies a hard truth: Not all who are physically alive will enjoy the spiritual Life given by God—only those who live in the Light of Jesus. For it is in His Light that we find Life.

Before You Meet:

Spend some time familiarizing yourself with the stories you will be investigating. Read John 2:13–3:21. This section covers the story of Jesus driving out the money changers from the temple and the story of Jesus' encounter with Nicodemus, a Pharisee.

To Begin Your Meeting:

Read this week's headline and then John 3:5-10 out loud. Invite Jesus to join you and answer some questions. Thankfully acknowledge that His Spirit is present as your Helper to guide your discussion. Please do not let this become some kind of ritual prayer. Remember, it is an actual invitation.

To Begin Your Discussion:

Read the following introduction out loud to the group:

In Chapter 1, John introduces us to Jesus, the Creator and Light of the world, the leader of a radical spiritual movement, and the founder of a new nation who would give His own life to deliver us from spiritual slavery. We immediately find Jesus zealously defending the integrity of His house and cleverly exposing the real problem with religious Israel in a clandestine meeting with Nicodemus, a key Jewish religious leader. John wrote as the disciple perhaps closest to Jesus (John 21:20-25), and in these two stories, he gives us a clear look at the passionate love of Jesus for His Father and indeed for the whole world. Why did Jesus have such an issue with "religious" life?

Discuss the Following Questions One at a Time.

Read each question out loud and listen to what each person is saying. Don't forget to ask your own questions to clarify and develop ideas together as a group. Help each other stay on topic with the reminder, "What does this have to do with the question we are discussing?"

1. Why was Jesus so angry about what the temple had become?

2. What does the temple represent in Jesus' day and how does Jesus' zeal for "His house" still continue today?

3. How does John use the story of Nicodemus to expose a fundamental problem with religion and introduce us to the heart of God for His world? Why was it impossible for a religious system to give Life?

4. How does this influence your understanding of what it means to have life in Jesus?

Note some of the ideas that strike you as especially meaningful.

Before you leave, share one or two of these ideas with the group. Read back important highlights from the previous week and add ideas from the current discussion. It is essential that you take a few minutes to do this before you break up the meeting. Continue circulating the notes. Use your text group or other social media tools to raise additional questions for further discussion but try not to get too far off the main subject. Don't forget that keeping a journal for yourself is also helpful.

Close with a prayer of thanksgiving and expectation that God will continue to show you more.

Within a day or two of your discussion, take at least one 15-minute time-out to allow Jesus to have easy access to your heart.

Sit comfortably, close your eyes, with no phone, no Bible, and no notepad. This is a time for you to just be in the presence of Jesus. Always begin by inviting the Holy Spirit to speak. Let thoughts go past you as you use this as sacred time with God. This is spiritual listening, and quiet is the sound of Jesus connecting with your soul, not your conscious mind. Remember that your subconscious mind is working, and your spirit is responding whether you are conscious of it or not.

Don't forget to be patient and cut yourself some slack. If there is a lot of noise in your head, try using your "sacred word" or phrase from a favorite song to call yourself back from the chaos!

Week 3 Headline:

Puzzling First Moves By Jesus Cause Confusion Among His Followers

I don't like causing disruption unless absolutely necessary. Traditions and standards are important to me. I believe they were important to Jesus as well, but He seemed more than willing to do whatever was necessary to achieve His mission, even if it meant upsetting some people. For example, He starts His own baptismal ministry instead of joining John's. This results in some misunderstood competition. John's disciples are anxious to defend him, but in this story, we hear that John the Baptist is joyful about turning the focus to Jesus. He realizes that his work, which started out as a ministry of repentance and purification (represented by his baptism), was now turning into a ministry about eternal Life found exclusively in Jesus and His baptism. John the Baptist knew it was time for his work to decrease and for the work of Jesus to increase.

Jesus is aware of the confusion He has caused. But He keeps right on going in what seemed like another impulsive decision. He journeys through Samaria to return home with another agenda. It was time to show the disciples what could truly unite and restore the nation, and this meant getting off the beaten path of tribal prejudice. At the well of Jacob, the site where the twelve tribes of Israel (Jacob) last stood together to receive the blessing of God, Jesus offers an even greater blessing to an unsuspecting Samaritan woman. Instead of water from a well that saved a nation, Jesus offers living water now flowing from His own Life to the world. He starts with a Samaritan woman who had lost all hope of security and now lived in a city of refuge.

I'm sure I would be as confused as the disciples when they returned from the village with food. They find Jesus already offering food to a crowd of Samaritans gathered to listen to this woman! Much to the surprise of his disciples, this woman became the start of a spiritual revival that changed the whole region! The disciples only needed to open their eyes and see that it was God Himself who was at work preparing fields like this one in Samaria for the harvest. What a fantastic picture for them to see. The great "I AM" of their once united nation was reaching the remnants of the nation with His living water!

Before You Meet:

Spend some time familiarizing yourself with the stories you will be investigating. Read John 3:22–4:42. This covers most of the story of Jesus' early ministry and the story of Jesus meeting a Samaritan woman at Jacob's well.

To Begin Your Meeting:

Read this week's headline and then John 4:9-10 out loud. Invite Jesus to join you and answer some questions. Thankfully acknowledge that His Spirit is present as your Helper to guide your discussion. Please do not let this become some kind of ritual prayer. Remember, it is an actual invitation.

To Begin Your Discussion:

Read the following introduction out loud to the group:

Jesus seemed to operate out of a different playbook than everyone else. Instead of working directly with John the Baptist, He starts His own ministry. Instead of going to the hub of the religious world in Jerusalem, He goes to Samaria. What was Jesus up to?

Discuss the Following Questions One at a Time.

Read each question out loud and listen to what each person is saying. Don't forget to ask your own questions to clarify and develop ideas together as a group. Help each other stay on topic with the reminder, "What does this have to do with the question we are discussing?"

1. How is the theme of "Life from above" (introduced in the story of Nicodemus) carried forward in the story of John the Baptist stepping behind Jesus and the story of the woman at the well?

2. What are the differences we are taught here between John's baptism for purification and Jesus' disciples baptizing His followers into eternal life? Why doesn't Jesus do the baptizing?

3. What did Jacob's well represent in the history of Israel and how did Jesus use this to tell His story of a new beginning for the world?

4. What was the key point the disciples—and all of us—need to hear?

Note some of the ideas that strike you as especially meaningful.

Before you leave, share one or two of these ideas with the group. Read back important highlights from the previous week and add ideas from the current discussion. It is essential that you take a few minutes to do this before you break up the meeting. Continue circulating the notes. Use your text group or other social media tools to raise additional questions for further discussion but try not to get too far off the main subject. Don't forget that keeping a journal for yourself is also helpful.

Close with a prayer of thanksgiving and expectation that God will continue to show you more.

Within a day or two of your discussion, take at least one 15-minute time-out to allow Jesus to have easy access to your heart.

Sit comfortably, close your eyes, with no phone, no Bible, and no notepad. This is a time for you to just be in the presence of Jesus. Always begin by inviting the Holy Spirit to speak. Let thoughts go past you as you use this as sacred time with God. This is spiritual listening, and quiet is the sound of Jesus connecting with your soul, not your conscious mind. Remember that your subconscious mind is working, and your spirit is responding whether you are conscious of it or not.

Don't forget to be patient and cut yourself some slack. If there is a lot of noise in your head, try using your "sacred word" or phrase from a favorite song to call yourself back from the chaos!

Week 4 Headline:

Is Jesus For or Against Miracles?

I have seen a few miracles in my life, and I have to say, it is not nearly as spooky or bizarre as it might sound. I am a bit embarrassed to say my first question was always, "Did I just witness a miracle?" In my defense, it was, after all, miraculous! In these stories, Jesus is expressing His power through the Holy Spirit to change the natural course of events from what seemed inevitable to what was humanly impossible! The purpose was always to show the love of God in a practical way.

It seems that John's purpose is to use these stories to expose the hard hearts of those who could only see Jesus as a miracle worker and not their loving Messiah. The story of a nobleman who pursues Jesus for the healing of his son with no idea of who He really is. The story of the healing of a lame man in a pagan temple who then turns Jesus in to the authorities for getting in his face about worshipping his false Greek gods. Or how about when Jesus feeds a crowd of over 5,000 only to be viewed as a human King who could do miracles like Moses rather than as their Messiah who was the Source of Life. Even His own disciples could not see Jesus as their Deliverer when He walked to them on the water in the storm.

The crowds begin to turn away from Jesus when He claims that *He* is the miracle that provides Life (the bread and water of Life). He was and is what they were looking for! But many only wanted the miracles, not the Source and the substance of the miracles they were seeking. Some believed in Jesus, but many did not. It was the beginning of a growing reluctance to embrace Jesus as the Messiah.

I have to admit, seeing God at work in visible ways is really exciting. But I must also be aware that He works far more in the invisible realm than anywhere else. I think followers of Jesus today can still be distracted by the sensationalism of miracles because miracles still happen! If we fail to see the love of Jesus in the miracle, we miss out on the real gift they give. We can and must boldly ask for miracles, but we must humbly submit our desires to the One who gives Life and love. Perhaps the greatest miracle of all is that Jesus can and will transform our hearts so we can see Him in our everyday lives!

Before You Meet:

Spend some time familiarizing yourself with the stories you will be investigating. Read John 4:43–6:71. This reading covers a variety of miracles performed by Jesus, including the healing of a Roman politician's son and a pagan lame man, feeding a Judean crowd of 5,000, and walking on the water during a storm!

To Begin Your Meeting:

Read this week's headline and then John 6:35-40 out loud. Invite Jesus to join you and answer some questions. Thankfully acknowledge that His Spirit is present as your Helper to guide your discussion. Please do not let this become some kind of ritual prayer. Remember, it is an actual invitation.

To Begin Your Discussion:

Read the following introduction out loud to the group:

We know from John's introduction that Jesus is the creator of Life and the founder and leader of a movement to restore Life to all humanity. We then find Him secretly trying to explain to Nicodemus that Life can only come "from above" where God Himself dwells—something Nicodemus should have known. This is followed by a surprise trip to Samaria where Jesus begins His mission among the lost tribes of Israel. There they see Him for who He really is—the Messiah—and they finally begin to take Him simply at His word.

In our study for today we find Jesus now working among the religiously faithful Judean tribes. Here He is less well-received. His miracles rather than His message become the focus. How would Jesus deal with their hardness of heart? Would He find a remnant of the faithful here?

Discuss the Following Questions One at a Time.

Read each question out loud and listen to what each person is saying. Don't forget to ask your own questions to clarify and develop ideas together as a group. Help each other stay on topic with the reminder, "What does this have to do with the question we are discussing?"

1. How does each story emphasize that the recipients of the miracles fail to see Jesus for who He is? How does this contrast with the story of the believers in Samaria?

2. Psalm 136 (especially verses 4-12) provides a great description of how Israel saw her Deliverer. How do these stories of Jesus' miracles clarify what they should have been seeking?

3. What is Jesus hoping that the crowds will see? How does this expand on the themes already introduced in the story of Nicodemus and the Samaritan woman at Jacob's well?

4. If we are honest with ourselves, what is it that we need to see to believe?

Note some of the ideas that strike you as especially meaningful.

Before you leave, share one or two of these ideas with the group. Read back important highlights from the previous week and add ideas from the current discussion. It is essential that you take a few minutes to do this before you break up the meeting. Continue circulating the notes. Use your text group or other social media tools to raise additional questions for further discussion but try not to get too far off the main subject. Don't forget that keeping a journal for yourself is also helpful.

Close with a prayer of thanksgiving and expectation that God will continue to show you more.

Within a day or two of your discussion, take at least one 15-minute time-out to allow Jesus to have easy access to your heart.

Sit comfortably, close your eyes, with no phone, no Bible, and no notepad. This is a time for you to just be in the presence of Jesus. Always begin by inviting the Holy Spirit to speak. Let thoughts go past you as you use this as sacred time with God. This is spiritual listening, and quiet is the sound of Jesus connecting with your soul, not your conscious mind. Remember that your subconscious mind is working, and your spirit is responding whether you are conscious of it or not.

Don't forget to be patient and cut yourself some slack. If there is a lot of noise in your head, try using your "sacred word" or phrase from a favorite song to call yourself back from the chaos!

Week 5 Headline:

Jesus' Credentials Disputed, but a Blind Man Sees It All

It's easy for me to believe that the people who doubted Jesus must have been a bit daft or at least more spiritually blind than the average human being to miss what was happening. But for the most part, members of "the crowd," as John calls them, were typical Jews going about their usual business. The supernatural events they were hearing about and seeing were upsetting the day-to-day routine and disturbing the fragile peace arrangement with the Roman Empire. No one seemed to know what it all meant, but whatever it was, it was not politically correct! It's no wonder that Jesus' credentials are called into question, helped along a bit by the antagonism of the popular and sinister pharisaical religious sect.

To deal with this, Jesus makes a public display of His credentials at the Feast of Tabernacles in Jerusalem (which paradoxically was a reenactment of God's provision for Israel on their journey to freedom through the wilderness). John's narrative provides us with a sort of study in unbelief. From the crowds, we hear doubt about Jesus' heritage, His education, His claims, His methods, His motives, and His purity. Even His sanity is questioned (John 7:19-20)! But at the end of the feast (which is celebrated by the pouring out of water from the pool of Siloam in the temple), Jesus proclaims Himself to be the source of the water that will soon flow from all who receive Him. This water will bring Life to the world as His Spirit pours out of the lives of His followers, not out of the temple!

Jesus knows that the doubts of these devoted Jews originated from unreliable earthly sources. He appeals to them with Truth directly from its source in heaven—His very own Father. This is the Truth that could set them free (John 8:31-32). But because of their loyalty to a corrupted religious system, the Truth that Jesus revealed became, in a very real sense, an obstacle to their freedom (John 8:45). There was simply no way around their doubts.

Jesus charges that their disloyalty to the God of their father Abraham would ultimately be their undoing. Once Jesus reveals that He actually met

Abraham, that Abraham was excited that Messiah's Day was coming (John 8:56), and that Jesus was in fact the "I Am" revealed to their fathers (John 8:58), the crowd turns murderous! Jesus escapes and soon after, performs one of the most profound miracles of His ministry—the story of the healing of the man blind from birth.

What made this miracle so meaningful was the obvious parallel to Israel's condition. Jesus, the Light of the world, sees a man born blind (like that generation of Israelites). His disciples (who seem to be MIA up to this point) can't help but ask who's to blame. Jesus turns their thinking upside down. He insists that the issue is not personal or generational sins (as they all thought). Why? Because man is not the center of this story; God's plan is! Here is their chance to see God display His plan at work: opening the eyes of the blind (John 9:3-5).

In a beautiful reminder of the creation story, Jesus first applies a mudpack (remember how God created Adam?) and then sends the man (who is still blind and covered in mud) to the pool of water in the temple court to wash (the pool of living water to which Jesus had just compared Himself). This man who never met Jesus is healed! By the time the man can see, Jesus is gone, and, of course, the Pharisees waste no time in once again criticizing Jesus for healing on the Sabbath.

But here is where it gets even more interesting. In the discussion that follows (John 9:26-34), the religious elites are exposed as frauds, who do their best to hide the evidence of God's work by ostracizing the man who was healed. They try to hide anything that would undermine their control. Jesus hears about it and goes to find the healed man who had seen the Light, just like He was hoping for Israel.

Are you ready for the punch line? Now that the blind man can see, he wants to know *who* to believe in, not *what* to believe! He wants to meet the One who delivered him from his miserable existence. No religious rules or theology needed. Standing face-to-face, Jesus introduces Himself as "the Son of Man" (the royal title of the Messiah). The once blind man already knows the concept of the "Son of Man" (his mind is working just fine even though he was blind). But now that he can see it is Jesus, the man believes and worships Him.

I love how John ties all these stories together. Starting with the story of the Samaritan woman at the well, then the interview with Nicodemus, the healing of the lame man at the pool of Bethesda, followed by miraculously feeding the crowds, then Jesus walking on the water, and ending with the healing of the man blind from birth—they all point us to Jesus as *the* Source of Life and the Deliverer of His people.

In the end, the man healed of his blindness acts out what Jesus hopes for all people: that all would believe and worship Him. These stories show us that failure to embrace Jesus produces a shame that only deepens disbelief. And this disbelief keeps us enslaved to our own ways. It's a vicious cycle only broken by the Light of Jesus.

Before You Meet:

Spend some time familiarizing yourself with the story you will be investigating. Read John 7:1–9:41. The main story for this week is the healing of the man blind from birth in John 9. Chapters 7 and 8 are important because they provide a build up to it.

To Begin Your Meeting:

Read this week's headline and then John 9:1-4, 35-38 out loud. Invite Jesus to join you and answer some questions. Thankfully acknowledge that His Spirit is present as your Helper to guide your discussion. Please do not let this become some kind of ritual prayer. Remember, it is an actual invitation.

To Begin Your Discussion:

Read the following introduction out loud to the group:

After His major success in Samaria and trouble at the temple in Jerusalem, Jesus retreats to spend most of His time around the Sea of Galilee. But dissention about His claims to be the Source of Life (the bread and water they must eat and drink) left Jesus with only a remnant of followers. He ends up at home in Nazareth with His family, and even they are unsure about Him. In our story today, Jesus secretly makes his way to the temple in Jerusalem for the feast of Tabernacles (John 7:10). The disciples seem strangely absent as the public discourse about Jesus gets more heated in Jerusalem. Why does Jesus intentionally subject Himself to public scrutiny yet again?

Discuss the Following Questions One at a Time.

Read each question out loud and listen to what each person is saying. Don't forget to ask your own questions to clarify and develop ideas together as a group. Help each other stay on topic with the reminder, "What does this have to do with the question we are discussing?"

1. How does the Feast of the Tabernacles provide an ironic context for John's discussion of unbelief? You may want to do a search with the title Feast of Tabernacles for some background information.

2. How does Jesus defend His role as Deliverer during the legal argument with the Pharisees in the temple?

3. What is the real problem keeping Israel from seeing Jesus for who He really is?

4. How does the story of the healing of the blind man reveal the way Jesus works in the world today?

Note some of the ideas that strike you as especially meaningful.

Before you leave, share one or two of these ideas with the group. Read back important highlights from the previous week and add ideas from the current discussion. It is essential that you take a few minutes to do this before you break up the meeting. Continue circulating the notes. Use your text group or other social media tools to raise additional questions for further discussion but try not to get too far off the main subject. Don't forget that it is also helpful to keep a journal for yourself.

Close with a prayer of thanksgiving and expectation that God will continue to show you more.

Within a day or two of your discussion, take at least one 15-minute time-out to allow Jesus to have easy access to your heart.

Sit comfortably, close your eyes, with no phone, no Bible, and no notepad. This is a time for you to just be in the presence of Jesus. Always begin by inviting the Holy Spirit to speak. Let thoughts go past you as you use this as sacred time with God. This is spiritual listening, and quiet is the sound of Jesus connecting with your soul, not your conscious mind. Remember that your subconscious mind is working, and your spirit is responding whether you are conscious of it or not.

Don't forget to be patient and cut yourself some slack. If there is a lot of noise in your head, try using your "sacred word" or phrase from a favorite song to call yourself back from the chaos!

Week 6 Headline:

Jesus Confronts A Failed Religious System With The Story Of A Good Shepherd

I love it when a story comes together! It's that moment when surprise twists and mysterious references suddenly become clear, and it all makes sense. This section in John is like that, but it takes a bit of Jewish backstory to see it. By the time of these events, Jesus has been challenging the religious elite of Israel for over a year. Now His confrontation with them gets right to the point. He "tells them plainly," just as they asked!

In the confrontation leading up to this, Jesus accuses the religious leaders of Jerusalem of being blind—as He heals a man blind from birth to illustrate His point. In this story, He accuses these leaders of being thieves and illegitimate priests by claiming that He is the promised *Good* Shepherd (not bad like the rest of them)! Jesus makes it clear that the restoration of the temple and Jewish religious order in Jerusalem after the Maccabean revolt (celebrated at the Feast of Dedication, which is the setting for this story) was of no value at all because of the corruption of the religious elite.

Jesus claims that His Father had chosen Him to be the One Shepherd, the Good Shepherd, to make things right by uniting the remnant of faithful Israelites with the new flocks of Gentiles into one flock. Jesus had the one Voice that *all* the lost sheep could hear. He would tend to the wounded, heal the sick, and protect the flock from the world full of enemies so that it could flourish. But more than that, Jesus would fight for His flock, not just comfort and make them feel secure. Indeed, He would die for them!

All other pretenders would ultimately be eliminated, leaving Jesus as the final Shepherd King. He was the promised One who fights for His followers as a Davidic ruler and the One who intercedes for them as the great High Priest. There was to be One Shepherd, not many, and one united flock; one King and one Kingdom united under Him. The nation of Israel at that time had neither, thanks to the blindness and hypocrisy of its religious leaders.

But how could Jesus be the *human* Davidic King, the Good Shepherd, and also be one with the heavenly Father as He claimed? The Pharisees had simply never considered the possibility that God and man would literally come together to fulfill these prophesies. Jesus' claim to be God was a capital offence, but His claim to be this God-Man was preposterous. To defend Himself, He refers to Psalm 82, which pictures humans as divine beings at the heavenly counsel table with God where they act as judges under His rule! Clearly, Jesus says, man is designed to coexist with and express the image of God. Jesus was claiming that as a man fully submitted to His Father, He was perfectly expressing the image of His Father. Jesus knew the importance of being human (please note my previous book by this title for more reading on this). In fact, He was more human than any other human being since the fall of man! The religious leaders could not cope with the insinuation that they were far less.

To illustrate Jesus' qualifications as the Good Shepherd, John gives us three unique, memorable stories. When Jesus raises Lazarus from the dead (literally calling him out of his grave), we get a glimpse of His authority, expressed in deep empathy for His close group of friends (remember Jesus weeping?). When questioned by Martha about His delay, Jesus doesn't criticize. He simply makes it clear that He didn't come to *do* resurrections (like some sort of miraculous stunt to show His power); He *is* resurrection and Life. He has authority over life and death because of who He is. He shows us He is the *GOOD* Shepherd, intervening to restore one of the sheep to show His Father's glory!

In the second story, Jesus returns for a visit to Bethany (a settlement for the poor) to celebrate Passover just a few days before His betrayal. At this celebration, He allows Mary to anoint His feet with valuable oil. John tells the story with an emphasis on the dignity and love demonstrated by Mary using her hair (culturally representing her honor) to wipe His feet. Rather than the symbolic preparation for His royal burial as in the anointing that followed a few days later at a different place (told in Matthew 26:6-13), Jesus receives Mary's gift so that all (except for Judas) could enjoy the moment as the fragrance of her gift filled the room. Truly, this was a place of intimate worship!

In the third story, we find Jesus welcomed into Jerusalem as the conquering King, coming in peace as a virtuous ruler to unite His people. Every man, woman, and child along His path are shouting, "Hosanna!"[2] to Jesus without realizing He had yet to finish His work. The new Kingdom would require His death and also, as He points out to them, their own.

To wrap it all up, John recalls the voice of God verifying that Jesus is indeed the glory of God revealed to all the world (Jews and Greeks). He repeats the central themes of Jesus as the light of the world and the source of eternal life. John reminds us all that Jesus is replacing a broken religious system with a path of sacrificial love.

I sometimes get a little lost in a long and nuanced story like this. Each time I read it, it seems to get a little richer. But maybe that's the point! As Jesus counts down the days to His betrayal and death, we hear His Voice getting nearer and clearer, calling His lost sheep together into His new Kingdom. I bet John is smiling as he writes this!

Before You Meet:

Spend some time familiarizing yourself with the stories you will be investigating. Read John 10:1–12:50. You will need to read Ezekial 34:1-24 and Ezekiel 37:24-27 to understand the significance of this passage to John's readers. You will note as you read that prophesies from Isaiah and Zechariah also feature prominently (see Isaiah 6 and Zechariah 9:9-12).

I realize this is quite a long section. It includes the story of the Good Shepherd, raising Lazarus from the dead, the anointing of Jesus' feet, and His royal entrance into Jerusalem on a donkey. I believe you will enjoy exploring the richness of these very familiar passages by seeing them together in a new light.

To Begin Your Meeting:

Read this week's headline and then John 10:8-15, 27-30, 11:25-27, 12:32-36, 44-46 out loud. It may be helpful to highlight or circle these verses ahead of time to make it easier to read smoothly. Invite Jesus to join you and answer some questions. Thankfully acknowledge that His Spirit is present as your

---

[2] A word that historically implied a submissive welcome to the conquering King.

Helper to guide your discussion. Please do not let this become some kind of ritual prayer. Remember, it is an actual invitation.

To Begin Your Discussion:

Read the following introduction out loud to the group:

The "shepherds" of Israel (her priests) had a long history of failure to protect and guide Israel in their relationship with the one God who reigned above all others (Ezekial 34:1-24). In Jesus' day, the problems had only gotten worse. The temple was a place of business, and the religious leaders were hypocrites, scoundrels, and blind to the spiritual needs of the people. Jesus contrasts Himself with the religious leaders of the day, drawing on the prophetic images of the Davidic Shepherd King spoken of in Ezekiel 37:24-27. How will Jesus confront the failure of their whole religious system?

Discuss the Following Questions One at a Time.

Read each question out loud and listen to what each person is saying. Don't forget to ask your own questions to clarify and develop ideas together as a group. Help each other stay on topic with the reminder, "What does this have to do with the question we are discussing?"

1. Jesus uses the metaphorical language of the Old Testament priesthood to compare Himself with Israel's bad shepherds. What was so good about the Good Shepherd?

2. How does Jesus defend this claim of being one with the heavenly Father without denying His earthly humanity? (This refers to John 10:30-37. Read Psalm 82 and Exodus 22:8-9 where human judges are referred to as *Elohim,* for comparison.)

3. How is the authority of Jesus' priestly role illustrated by the stories at the resurrection of Lazarus, the anointing of His feet by Mary, and the entry into Jerusalem riding on the donkey?

4. What should we expect of Jesus in our world as the fulfillment of Israel's promised Davidic King of peace and Good Shepherd?

Note some of the ideas that strike you as especially meaningful.

Before you leave, share one or two of these ideas with the group. Read back important highlights from the previous week and add ideas from the current discussion. It is essential that you take a few minutes to do this before you break up the meeting. Continue circulating the notes. Use your text group or other social media tools to raise additional questions for further discussion but try not to get too far off the main subject. Don't forget that keeping a journal for yourself is also helpful.

Close with a prayer of thanksgiving and expectation that God will continue to show you more.

Within a day or two of your discussion, take at least one 15-minute time-out to allow Jesus to have easy access to your heart.

Sit comfortably, close your eyes, with no phone, no Bible, and no notepad. This is a time for you to just be in the presence of Jesus. Always begin by inviting the Holy Spirit to speak. Let thoughts go past you as you use this as sacred time with God. This is spiritual listening, and quiet is the sound of Jesus connecting with your soul, not your conscious mind. Remember that your subconscious mind is working, and your spirit is responding whether you are conscious of it or not.

Don't forget to be patient and cut yourself some slack. If there is a lot of noise in your head, try using your "sacred word" or phrase from a favorite song to call yourself back from the chaos!

Digging deeper into the story of the man behind the mystery of Life

Key question:

How and why does Jesus give Life? In what ways does Jesus help us see what Life really is? Why does this require faith?

Discuss this statement:

We see in Jesus a man who was willing to give His life in total obedience to the mission of His Father. We know little of early days other than His miraculous birth, His family trade, and His informal self-training in the teachings of Moses and the prophets. What sort of man would live His life like this?

To prepare for your next and final feature story:

Consider the following questions: The stories of the Gospel of John give us a picture of the nature and character of Jesus. We get to know Him as the loving Good Shepherd of Israel whose flock would come from all over the world. What did He expect would be different about life for His sheep in His fold once they were rescued from the world? What was His personal agenda for His followers?

Feature Story #5:

Jesus Personally Leads the Way to Our Restoration

How far is Jesus willing to go to give us what we need to live?

Welcome to the fifth and final feature story in your guided journey through the Gospels! It has been an incredible journey through the life and teachings of Jesus. These last five weeks will wrap things up by looking at how Jesus launches the greatest Kingdom in human history. It's not a political system or a religious institution. It's not an ideology or a moral code. It's a family of followers from every race and nation immersed in the Life of the resurrected Jesus, filled and led by His Holy Spirit to live as His partners in restoring life to the world.

You already know what kind of man Jesus was, how the events of His life and His teachings all culminated in a final lifesaving death and lifegiving resurrection. Now you will pick up where we left off in the stories of John to investigate His final meetings, parting words, final act of love, and the promises made to His followers to see what kind of leader Jesus actually is.

These stories told by John have been a source of hope and inspiration for thousands of years and I believe are a fitting conclusion to challenge each of us to embrace Jesus and His mission.

Week 7 Headline:

Jesus' Final Dinner With His Disciples Turns Serious

It's hard to imagine myself wrapping up three years of ministry with a small group of people, with my betrayal and execution just hours away! What would I say? How would I say it? As He gathers with His inner circle of followers for a last meal, Jesus clearly wants to be sure they see the big picture of who He is, where He came from, and where He is going. But at the same time, His main concern seems to be for their immediate welfare. There is no hint of Jesus feeling sorry for Himself or feeling doubtful about the future. He seems confident He has accomplished what He set out to do in perfect alignment with His Father. But now it will be up to them! They will need each other and a sense of hope and confidence that this is not an ending but just the beginning of what the Father has begun through His Son.

Jesus knows exactly how to wrap up their time together. His farewell message reveals with stunning clarity just what they will need to persevere in their faith. Jesus acts out the first part of His message to them. They see that they will need to be there for each other, washing each other's feet just like Jesus washed theirs to remove the grime of daily life. Ceremonial cleansing will no longer be needed—only the humility to engage in the nitty gritty of life with one another.

Second, they will need a new commandment, a new focus for their obedience. The great commandments of the Old Covenant—to love God and love neighbor as self—could now be defined by the love of Jesus for His Father and for His disciples. Jesus could ask them to "love one another as I have loved you." Now the disciples had a model to follow, not just words. And not just a model either. With this new command, they actually *receive* love from Jesus to give to others rather than just loving their neighbor as themselves. Judas is used as the perfect example of the kind of love they must have for each other, even those who would betray them. Jesus says "someone" will betray Him, but the actual betrayer (Judas) is honored with the same foot washing and the last piece of broken bread at Jesus' side before he is sent on his way, with no hint from

Jesus that he is the betrayer. Only later do the other disciples find out that they are not the ones, though they have the humility to realize it could have been any one of them. (Let him who stands take heed lest he fall!)

Finally, they needed a complete picture of the mission. Jesus shifts the disciples' attention to their relationship with His Father. Jesus reminds them that just as they have loved Him, now they must love the Father. The focus is not on *where* Jesus is going (though this seems their main concern) but *who* He is going to. He wants them to see that His relationship with His Father holds the key for their future and, in fact, has been key to His whole mission all along. Jesus reminds them that He is the Source of Life, which flows directly from His Father to them. *They* are the sheep He was given by His Father, and He will keep them and give His life for them as the Good Shepherd. Jesus is the Way to the Father (remember the shepherd acts as the door to the fold), the Truth about the Father, and the Life from the Father.

Jesus assures them they will not be left as orphans—quite the opposite! He promises to ask His Father to send the Holy Spirit once He returns home. And His Spirit will ensure they are part of His new spiritual family! In fact, they will experience a true spiritual resurrection in their lifetimes, not one they have to wait for at the end of time as they had been taught in their Jewish tradition. Because Jesus returns to His Father as a living, resurrected human being, they would have access to all the riches found in God simply by *living* in Jesus' name (asking for whatever they will).

For the disciples, I think it was a bit of the "have your cake and eat it, too" dilemma. If Jesus stayed, then He did not go to His Father. If He did not go to His Father, He could not complete His mission and release the resources of heaven for His followers. I would hate to give up walking day to day with Jesus, but living for Jesus after He returns to His Father just might be better! It sets the stage for the opportunity to share the glory He receives when He returns home!

Before You Meet:

Spend some time familiarizing yourself with the story you will be investigating. Read John 13:1–14:31. Note that these verses provide just the first part of John's recounting of the events of the Last Supper, which goes all the way through John 17.

To Begin Your Meeting:

Read this week's headline and then John 13:3-5, 14-15, 34-35, and 14:12-21, 27 out loud. Because of the number of verses, my suggestion is to mark these verses in your Bible before the meeting so it will be easier to read through them with as little interruption in flow as possible. Invite Jesus to join you to help answer some questions and thankfully acknowledge that His Spirit is present as your Helper to guide your discussion.

To Begin Your Discussion:

Read the following introduction out loud to the group:

John does not portray Jesus' final meal before His crucifixion as some kind of pep rally or CEO speech about coming success. These final events only seem to drive home the point that Jesus is going away. Only later is it clear that this final meeting was the turning point for the first followers of Jesus.

This week we begin the investigation of Jesus' final days with His disciples before His death by looking into His farewell message. I believe it is full of clues that begin to unravel the mystery of why Jesus did what He did. What does Jesus' message, just hours before His betrayal, tell us about the nature of His divine love?

Discuss the Following Questions One at a Time.

Read each question out loud and listen to what each person is saying. Don't forget to ask your own questions to clarify and develop ideas together as a group. Help each other stay on topic with the reminder, "What does this have to do with the question we are discussing?"

1. John picks up the story of the Last Supper during the after-dinner conversation. How does the foot washing demonstrate the kind of life the disciples must lead once He leaves?

2.   Why does no one realize that it is Judas who will betray Jesus? What do Jesus' actions towards Him demonstrate?

3.   What is the significance of the "new" commandment (to love one another) compared to the "great" commandments of the law (to love your neighbor as yourself)?

4.   Why does Jesus focus the disciples on His relationship with His Father?

Note some of the ideas that strike you as especially meaningful.

Before you leave, share one or two of these ideas with the group. Read back important highlights from the previous week and add ideas from the current discussion. It is essential that you take a few minutes to do this before you break up the meeting. Continue circulating the notes. Don't forget to use your text group or other social media tools to raise additional questions for further discussion but try not to get too far off the main subject. Don't forget that keeping a journal for yourself is also helpful.

Close with a prayer of thanksgiving and expectation that God will continue to show you more.

Within a day or two of your discussion, take at least one 15-minute time-out to allow Jesus to have easy access to your heart.

Sit comfortably, close your eyes, with no phone, no Bible, and no notepad. This is a time for you to just be in the presence of Jesus. Always begin by inviting the Holy Spirit to speak. Let thoughts go past you as you use this as sacred time with God. This is spiritual listening, and quiet is the sound of Jesus connecting with your soul, not your conscious mind. Remember that your subconscious mind is working, and your spirit is responding whether you are conscious of it or not.

Don't forget to be patient and cut yourself some slack. If there is a lot of noise in your head, try using your "sacred word" or phrase from a favorite song to call yourself back from the chaos!

Week 8 Headline:

Jesus Guides His Disciples Through The Greatest Ever Spiritual Transition In History

I really don't like change. It's one of those things I know is needed but try to avoid. I think Jesus' disciples knew change was coming and had no idea how to handle it. The disciples needed to know how to relate to His Father now that He was leaving. Jesus uses a very simple image to encourage them. On one hand, abiding in Him like the branches of a vine is a simple analogy. But to the disciples, the Vine was more than an agricultural comparison; it was a radical description of a new position with the Father of Israel.

Drawing on an Old Testament analogy, Jesus explains that His new Kingdom is like a new and more expansive Israel, with many branches connected to the "true" Vine rather than many vines growing from Jacob (Isaiah 5:1-7). The unrepentant Israel would have to be discarded in the fire as Isaiah had prophesied, but the new branches from every nation in the world would bear fruit and be pruned by His Father to bear even more fruit than they could ever imagine (blessing the world with justice and righteousness)!

But what does "abiding" mean? Jesus explains that the disciples must learn to find their Life *in* Him not just in what they learned *about* Him. They could no longer be comforted by their beliefs about Jesus—they must be strengthened by their faith in Him. The good news was that if they loved as Jesus loved them, they would not just survive—they could thrive! The Father would send them the Help they needed to carry on the mission of Jesus as full *partners* in His work, not just participants in a training project. And not only that, but they were also now free to ask the Father for anything in His name—anything! As crazy as it may have seemed at the time, the disciples came to see that they were clean, loved, welcomed, empowered, and glorified by this new arrangement.

The Vine was a great picture of how this all flowed from His Father. The great "I Am" made it clear who they were. They go from God's image bearers to fruit bearers, from being servants to being friends, from being participants in a mission to being partners with Jesus in His ongoing work. This would be the transition from an Old Covenant relationship with the Father to a New Covenant relationship. They would go from a religious system to loving from a heart transformed by the Spirit of God just as God had promised long ago (Jeremiah 31:31)!

I love the realism in Jesus' words. The disciples will have deep sorrow, they will weep, they do not yet know everything they need to know . . . in fact, Jesus knows they do not even have the capacity to bear it! They will doubt, and they will be scattered. But they will succeed! Today, as a result of their miraculous faithfulness, we are each one of the branches. Though we have not personally experienced the historical transition from Old to New Covenant, we most certainly benefit from it now. We have each transitioned from darkness to Light, from death to Life, from participant to partner. And we, too, must continue to abide in the true Vine on our journey, loving one another as He has loved us, asking whatever we want from our loving and gracious Father. The world will make it difficult for us, but if we cling to the Vine, we need not fear. We can cheerfully and confidently say, "Jesus has overcome the world!"

Before You Meet:

Spend some time familiarizing yourself with the story you will be investigating. Read John 15:1–16:33. It is a continuation of Jesus' farewell message to the disciples.

To Begin Your Meeting:

Read this week's headline and then John 15:1-8 out loud. Invite Jesus to join you and answer some questions. Thankfully acknowledge that His Spirit is present as your Helper to guide your discussion. Please do not let this become some kind of ritual prayer. Remember, it is an actual invitation.

To Begin Your Discussion:

Read the following introduction out loud to the group:

The dinner conversation with Jesus and His symbolic gesture to wash their feet make it clear that huge change is coming. As they leave the Upper Room for the evening under a cloud of self-doubt about who will betray Him, Jesus has some final words to encourage and direct them. What will Jesus say to prepare His disciples for the challenge of a lifetime?

Discuss the Following Questions One at a Time.

Read each question out loud and listen to what each person is saying. Don't forget to ask your own questions to clarify and develop ideas together as a group. Help each other stay on topic with the reminder, "What does this have to do with the question we are discussing?"

1. Why does Jesus expand on several specific themes from His Last Supper message (last week's story)? What changes will the disciples soon be experiencing because Jesus is physically leaving them?

2. How does the analogy of the Vine connect with God's story of Israel as a vineyard (Isaiah 5:1-7)? What new truths does Jesus add in His version of the story? What does Jesus see as the key to managing the incredible changes that are coming soon?

3. What does Jesus mean by inviting us to "abide" in Him? Based on Isaiah 5:7, what is the fruit Jesus expects from His followers who are abiding? How does the Father's pruning help us bear more fruit?

4. In what ways does Jesus see the work of the Holy Spirit as enabling a new partnership with His followers? What does Jesus mean by asking anything of the Father in His name?

Note some of the ideas that strike you as especially meaningful.

Before you leave, share one or two of these ideas with the group. Read back important highlights from the previous week and add ideas from the current discussion. It is essential that you take a few minutes to do this before you break up the meeting. Continue circulating the notes. Don't forget to use your text group or other social media tools to raise additional questions for further discussion but try not to get too far off the main subject. Don't forget that keeping a journal for yourself is also helpful.

Close with a prayer of thanksgiving and expectation that God will continue to show you more.

Within a day or two of your discussion, take at least one 15-minute time-out to allow Jesus to have easy access to your heart.

Sit comfortably, close your eyes, with no phone, no Bible, and no notepad. This is a time for you to just be in the presence of Jesus. Always begin by inviting the Holy Spirit to speak. Let thoughts go past you as you use this as sacred time with God. This is spiritual listening, and quiet is the sound of Jesus connecting with your soul, not your conscious mind. Remember that your subconscious mind is working, and your spirit is responding whether you are conscious of it or not.

Don't forget to be patient and cut yourself some slack. If there is a lot of noise in your head, try using your "sacred word" or phrase from a favorite song to call yourself back from the chaos!

Week 9 Headline:

Will The Prayers Of Jesus Be Enough To Turn The Tide Of Evil In Our World?

I don't use the word "glory" very often. It's not part of my conversational vocabulary. The fact is, I have a hard time defining it. Even today as I read Jesus' prayer for glory, I am a bit baffled. It's hard to imagine this was what Jesus ultimately expected to come from His time on earth.

The final pages of Jesus' story reveal that a momentous change in the spiritual world was just ahead. Jesus prays with words that allow His disciples to see these changes in a new light. You may recall that the children of Israel were hoping for the glory of God to fill the temple (the Shekinah glory). They were hoping that if they finished rebuilding the Jerusalem temple a second time, God would return to free them from their enemies. But Jesus saw His work in a much larger context, a context that stretched back in time to before the world began. The eternal glory of God was going to be unveiled for the world to see once again! There would be no pillar of fire over the temple—no power confined to a building or a place. How was the glory of God to be revealed? Clearly, not the way they thought.

The truth of it all comes out in the prayer of Jesus. It was time for the whole story about Jesus to be revealed so that He and His Father would be celebrated and revered around the world. The glory of God would not just fill the temple; it would fill the whole earth because Jesus was soon to be given full authority to restore spiritual Life to mortal flesh. The Life Jesus had experienced for all eternity with His Father, the Life that had been breathed into human beings at our creation, was again to be poured into human beings like rivers of Living Water. Those belonging to God, the great I Am, would now experience Him as Abba, the Father-God who is present in their lives. The glory that was displayed in the relationship between the Father and the Son since before the world even existed would now be poured out on the whole earth through the lives of those who followed Jesus!

The disciples grew up in a culture not allowed to even speak the name of God. Now they are invited to ask anything in the name of God. Indeed, they are invited to live in His Name. They must come to believe that the unapproachable God whose glory once filled the temple now lives among them. They've heard His Voice and seen His works revealed in Jesus. Now, they are assigned to be His representatives. As Jesus prepares to return to His Father, He asks the Father to move forward with the plan to reveal His glory in a new way.

Jesus hands the disciples back to His Father to protect and unite them. But this "unity" was not about uniformity. It was not about losing their distinctiveness as individuals—but about enhancing it! Like pieces of a divine puzzle, their lives would together tell a new story of God's presence and glory on earth. As Paul would later say, it is like parts of a body coming together as a unit representing the presence of God on the earth. We know that soon after the resurrection, the Father sends the Holy Spirit to take up residence in their lives, and they even see the Shekinah glory on each other's heads. It seems that Jesus was asking His Father to build a new "temple" made from the lives of all those specially chosen by Him. He would unite them for the sole purpose of revealing His glory to the world! What a privilege!

As I look at the religious world today, I see we are a long way from this unity and displaying this glory. Tragically we are consumed with the idea of building religious empires (which, by the way, was why God confused human language at the tower of Babel). Our Father has no interest in that. It shrinks His glory down. It trivializes what He has poured into us as the human race.

But there is light in our world. If I look at those who love and wholeheartedly follow Jesus, there is something beautiful and glorious there for the world to see. There is a unity of mind and spirit that crosses cultural, denominational, and socioeconomic boundaries. I've seen it shared between the poorest of the poor and the wealthy, between those who worship the way I do and those who worship differently. No matter your culture of origin, all followers of Jesus share a new cultural identity.

The first followers of Jesus didn't know it yet, but that final dinner meeting, with the discussion and prayer that followed, was the turning point for them. Jesus had to leave them to oversee the building of a new spiritual temple filled with His glory. He didn't come to stay. He came to build the foundation.

His Father would build the building. These disciples would go on to become the sacrificial leaders, abiding in Him, loving each other and the world as He did, united by a faith that revealed the Truth. They, and all the faithful who followed after, would become the temple filled with the glory of God for all to see.

We should not despair because of our own failures or the failure of our world and even our churches. Jesus' closing prayer for all His disciples is cause for hope! It is being answered with a solid YES by His Father. The prayer of Jesus *is* enough to turn the tide of evil in our world. Evil persists, but I don't bear the burden of solving the world's problems—He does. A faithful remnant continues to proclaim God's glory by sharing the things God does. The little things we each contribute become a huge wave when they are taken together! I will never see the whole picture; at best, I may see just a hint of the part that He has given me to play. But that is enough for the glory of God to be revealed and, in the end, to fill the earth like the waters fill the sea!

Before You Meet:

Spend some time familiarizing yourself with the story you will be investigating. Read John 17:1-26. It is one of the few recorded prayers of Jesus.

To Begin Your Meeting:

Read this week's headline and then John 17:1-5, 12, 20-23 out loud. Invite Jesus to join you and answer some questions. Thankfully acknowledge that His Spirit is present as your Helper to guide your discussion. Please do not let this become some kind of ritual prayer. Remember, it is an actual invitation.

To Begin Your Discussion:

Read the following introduction out loud to the group:

In the final hours of Jesus' life before the crucifixion, John recounts a meal, an act of service, a teaching on love, and finally, for today's discussion, a prayer. It is full of clues that can help us in our investigation of Jesus—the man behind the mission to restore the world as a Shepherd restores His flock. What does His final prayer with His disciples reveal about Him and His mission?

Discuss the Following Questions One at a Time.

Read each question out loud and listen to what each person is saying. Don't forget to ask your own questions to clarify and develop ideas together as a group. Help each other stay on topic with the reminder, "What does this have to do with the question we are discussing?"

1. Why does Jesus view eternal Life as a gift that only He has authority to give?

2. How is the mission of Jesus rooted in the glory given by the Father?

3. How is this prayer a statement of Jesus' ongoing commitment to us (see John 17:18-19)?

4. How does the glory we share with Jesus bring unity and represent victory (see John 17:22-23)?

Note some of the ideas that strike you as especially meaningful.

Before you leave, share one or two of these ideas with the group. Read back important highlights from the previous week and add ideas from the current discussion. It is essential that you take a few minutes to do this before you break up the meeting. Continue circulating the notes. Don't forget to use your text group or other social media tools to raise additional questions for further discussion but try not to get too far off the main subject. Don't forget that keeping a journal for yourself is also helpful.

Close with a prayer of thanksgiving and expectation that God will continue to show you more.

Within a day or two of your discussion, take at least one 15-minute time-out to allow Jesus to have easy access to your heart.

Sit comfortably, close your eyes, with no phone, no Bible, and no notepad. This is a time for you to just be in the presence of Jesus. Always begin by inviting the Holy Spirit to speak. Let thoughts go past you as you use this as sacred time with God. This is spiritual listening, and quiet is the sound of Jesus connecting with your soul, not your conscious mind. Remember that your subconscious mind is working, and your spirit is responding whether you are conscious of it or not.

Don't forget to be patient and cut yourself some slack. If there is a lot of noise in your head, try using your "sacred word" or phrase from a favorite song to call yourself back from the chaos!

Week 10 Headline:

Jesus Paves a Sure but Difficult Path to Life

It's been said that you never really know someone until you see how they respond to challenges. The betrayal, trial, torture, and death of Jesus were certainly that and then some. The unique responses of Jesus to the worst day of His life show us what love looks like. The One who said He would give His life for His sheep makes good on His promise. No compromise in His claims. No avoidance of reality. No hesitation to do what His Father asked of Him. The pain is real, the isolation on the cross—heartbreaking. Life, for which he claimed to be the source and guide, leaves His physical body (at least temporarily). Why? So He could set free those who put their faith in Him—free them from the curse of a failed religious system; free them from spiritual death to give them Life. Jesus' submission to His Father's plan was exactly what was needed to turn the spiritual realm upside down. It was not the pain He experienced that frees us—it was the love for us revealed in the pain that changed everything.

The submission of Jesus out of love for us and for His Father was essential for completion of His mission. But John makes sure we see Jesus from another equally important perspective: Jesus is portrayed as the real authority in each scene. At the Last Supper, Jesus honors His betrayer with the last piece of bread. He actually sends Judas out to betray Him. At His betrayal, the soldiers fall backwards at His Name, and Jesus scolds Peter for defending Him with a sword. During His sham trials before the religious and political authorities, Jesus is clear that He need not prove anything to anyone—the truth is His defense, and the authority is ultimately His Father's (John 19:11). Even on the cross, Jesus is named as the King, voluntarily giving up His life for the crimes of His people, not because of any guilt of His own. His final words are "It is finished," not "I give up." Jesus dies willingly as a King, not a slave.

After His death, prophecy about Him continues to unfold as His side is pierced. No bones are broken. He receives a royal burial. The massive curtain in the temple tears, stifling the hope of God ever returning there. The dead begin rising from their graves, not as ghosts but as real people. All these events demonstrate His power, even after His physical death. Then there is deafening silence for three long days . . . as the Passover goes by with no Jesus . . . and the disciples in fear that once the festival ends, so would their lives.

The reaction of the disciples to the news of the empty tomb only proves that their doubts remain unresolved. Despite the clarity of His promise to rise from the dead, no one thinks to take Jesus' promise to return after three days literally. They believe He has raised the dead, but how can He raise *Himself* from the dead? It is no surprise we hear them wondering, *Where did He go? Who took Him?*

Yet His Voice is clear and recognizable as He greets Mary in the garden. She clings to Him with joy, and Jesus shares the joyful news she must carry to the rest of the disciples: She has seen Jesus, and He is returning to the heavenly Father, who is now *their* Father as well. His God is their God. But the good news falls on deaf ears. They all doubt, not just Thomas. They all need to see His wounds to believe it's real. Once Jesus shows Himself to them, they all come to believe it, and they all receive the breath of Life from the resurrected Jesus. His Life would now be their Life through the Holy Spirit. Jesus' final words proclaim an encouragement to us now: "Blessed are those who have not seen but yet believe!"

Did Jesus carry the memory of all the pain in His resurrected body? I am sure He did. The trauma of those experiences became a deep well of empathy for humanity, a seal on the love that took Him from the cross to the throne. He remembers it still today. This is what qualifies Him to be our mediator, Priest, Good Shepherd, and our King, seated on the throne of a new Kingdom where we, His people, again can walk with our Creator.

I know our world is difficult and messy and uncertain. But life with Jesus just makes sense in some cosmic way. All the stories of the Gospels look forward to another day when there will be no physical barriers between the heavens and the earth. God's thrones will again be the center of the world, His divine council room will be available for the assembly of all the nations, and all the earth will be full of His glory. Evil will be gone never to return, as if it never existed, and Jesus will reign forever and ever. This is who Jesus is and why we can do no less than submit our lives to His. This is why we can do no more than to proclaim that He is worthy. I say, "Come quickly, Lord Jesus! Come quickly."

Before You Meet:

Spend some time familiarizing yourself with the teaching you will be investigating. Read all of John 18:1–20:18. This includes the story of Jesus' betrayal, His crucifixion, and resurrection. You have already investigated these events (Feature Story #1, Weeks 6 and 7), but John adds some important details and perspective not found in Matthew. If you have time, it would be worth looking back at those discussions.

To Begin Your Meeting:

Read this week's headline and then John 18:36-37 and John 20:11-18 out loud. Invite Jesus to join you and answer some questions. Thankfully acknowledge that His Spirit is present as your Helper to guide your discussion. Please do not let this become some kind of ritual prayer. Remember, it is an actual invitation.

To Begin Your Discussion:

Read the following introduction out loud to the group:

The path to the cross is certain; Jesus' commitment to completing His task is clear. All that remains is for the gruesome events to play out. John gives us some of the most memorable and beautiful descriptions of Jesus in the most difficult time of His life. What do we learn about Jesus when His life is at its worst?

Discuss the Following Questions One at a Time.

Read each question out loud and listen to what each person is saying. Don't forget to ask your own questions to clarify and develop ideas together as a group. Help each other stay on topic with the reminder, "What does this have to do with the question we are discussing?"

1. How does John make sure we see the full authority of Jesus in all the final events of His life?

2. What made the Good Shepherd so good?

3. What might be the significance of Jesus appearing to Mary as a gardener after His resurrection? What message does He give her?

4. Why did Jesus "breathe" on His disciples?

Note some of the ideas that strike you as especially meaningful.

Before you leave, share one or two of these ideas with the group. Read back important highlights from the previous week and add ideas from the current discussion. It is essential that you take a few minutes to do this before you break up the meeting. Continue circulating the notes. Use your text group or other social media tools to raise additional questions for further discussion but try not to get too far off the main subject. Don't forget that keeping a journal for yourself is also helpful.

Close with a prayer of thanksgiving and expectation that God will continue to show you more.

Within a day or two of your discussion, take at least one 15-minute time-out to allow Jesus to have easy access to your heart.

Sit comfortably, close your eyes, with no phone, no Bible, and no notepad. This is a time for you to just be in the presence of Jesus. Always begin by inviting the Holy Spirit to speak. Let thoughts go past you as you use this as sacred time with God. This is spiritual listening, and quiet is the sound of Jesus connecting with your soul, not your conscious mind. Remember that your subconscious mind is working, and your spirit is responding whether you are conscious of it or not.

Don't forget to be patient and cut yourself some slack. If there is a lot of noise in your head, try using your "sacred word" or phrase from a favorite song to call yourself back from the chaos!

Week 11 Headline:

A New Mission Begins

I've often wondered why the disciples seem to have such a hard time recognizing Jesus. After all, they have lived with Him for three years. But Mary thinks Jesus is a gardener, and the rest of the disciples don't recognize Him until He lets them touch His hands and side. A week later the same story with Thomas, who finally puts it into words: "My Lord and my God!" Sometime later, seven of the disciples follow Peter out fishing, where again they fail to recognize Jesus at first. All in all, it's not a great start to what is supposed to be a courageous mission. They have caught no fish, and Peter seems to try unsuccessfully to walk on water again once he hears it's Jesus. (Note, the disciples still don't seem to recognize Him, even once they get to shore, and seem embarrassed to ask.)

Just like He did when they first met, Jesus sends them out to fish on the right side of the boat, where their nets are filled with large fish; this time their nets remain strong and don't break. And it turns out Jesus doesn't even need the fish—they do! If they are going to have breakfast with Him, it's their catch that matters.

What a strange ending to an amazing journey! It seems they were learning to believe without seeing, just like all those who would come after them. There was no big sermon, no encouraging words—just some breakfast and a private conversation with Peter overheard by John. "Feed My sheep and follow Me," says Jesus. The other Gospel writers fill in more of the final events, but for John, this seems to be the beginning of his life-long journey with Jesus: Eating with Him at a simple meal He prepared on the beach, reflecting on the love he experienced, and learning to shepherd those who respond to the Voice of the Good Shepherd. For John and for us, I think there is no greater privilege.

Before You Meet:

Spend some time familiarizing yourself with the story you will be investigating. Read John 20:19–21:25. (Note that the formal ending of the

Gospel is probably John 20:31 with an epilogue that follows as Chapter 21.) Compare with John 8:42 and John 17:18.

To Begin Your Meeting:

Read this week's headline and then John 20:21-23 out loud. Invite Jesus to join you and answer some questions. Thankfully acknowledge that His Spirit is present as your Helper to guide your discussion. Please do not let this become some kind of ritual prayer. Remember, it is an actual invitation.

To Begin Your Discussion:

Read the following introduction out loud to the group:

John describes the first two appearances of Jesus after His resurrection. A third appearance is documented in John 21, probably by another author who worked closely with John. All three appearances seem to paint a picture of His final challenge to join Him as partners in the continuation of His mission.

Discuss the Following Questions One at a Time.

Read each question out loud and listen to what each person is saying. Don't forget to ask your own questions to clarify and develop ideas together as a group. Help each other stay on topic with the reminder, "What does this have to do with the question we are discussing?"

1. Jesus, Himself an "apostle,"[3] sends out[4] His disciples. He sends them out by "breathing" on them. What story does this remind you of in Genesis?

---

[3] Meaning "set apart" for a mission by His Father, as in John 5:36.
[4] "Sends out" is a different word in Greek, meaning dispatched with purpose to do His assignment, as in John 6:38.

2. Why is Jesus not easily recognizable after His resurrection? Who makes the first announcement to the disciples? Who does Thomas doubt? Why is this an important example for the future?

3. What is the significance of the fishing expedition (look back at the events as told in Luke 5:1-11 for comparison)? How does this experience show Jesus' blessing?

4. The final scene is a dialogue between Peter and Jesus with John watching. Why does Jesus commission Peter as a shepherd? Whose sheep was he to feed?

Note some of the ideas that strike you as especially meaningful.

Before you leave, share one or two of these ideas with the group. Read back important highlights from the previous week and add ideas from the current discussion. It is essential that you take a few minutes to do this before you break up the meeting. Continue circulating the notes. Don't forget to use your text group or other social media tools to raise additional questions for further discussion but try not to get too far off the main subject. Don't forget that keeping a journal yourself is also helpful.

Close with a prayer of thanksgiving and expectation that God will continue to show you more.

Within a day or two of your discussion, take at least one 15-minute time-out to allow Jesus to have easy access to your heart.

Sit comfortably, close your eyes, no phone, no Bible, and no notepad. This is a time for you to just be in the presence of Jesus. Always begin by inviting the Holy Spirit to speak. Let thoughts go past you as you use this as sacred time with God. This is spiritual listening, and quiet is the sound of Jesus connecting with your soul, not your conscious mind. Remember that your subconscious mind is working, and your spirit is responding whether you are conscious of it or not.

Don't forget to be patient and cut yourself some slack. If there is a lot of noise in your head, try using your "sacred word" or phrase from a favorite song to call yourself back from the chaos!

Digging Deeper Into Our Story Of Restoration

Key question:

If Jesus' primary mission was to begin the restoration of creation, what does it mean to be restored as human beings specifically?

Discuss this statement:

The stories of the Gospel of John give us a picture of the nature and character of Jesus. We get to know Him as the loving Good Shepherd of Israel whose flock would come from all over the world. What did He expect would be different about life for the sheep in His fold once they were rescued from the world? What was His personal agenda for His followers?

Epilogue

Final thoughts

A Mission Worth Dying For

You've come a long way in your investigation! Congratulations on the great work. You've covered humanity's new beginning, our path to restoration, an invisible spiritual domain that gives us sanctuary and hope, and the nature and character of Jesus—the man behind it all. He is the One who personally led the way to monumental changes in the spiritual domain, changes that opened the door for our restoration. Our five Feature Stories make it clear that there is hope, there is Light, and there is Life within our grasp—all because of Jesus.

There's no question about the Creator's love for us as the reason for all this: it's why Jesus came, why He sacrificed Himself, and why Life is offered as a gift received through faith, simply by believing in Him. (See Chapter 19 in *The Importance of Being Human.*) It's Truth worth sharing! But I think there is more to the story.

From the beginning of our study, we have been investigating the pieces of a magnificent narrative that for the modern Western mind is difficult to accept: The mystery of Life, hidden for ages by the darkness of human corruption and the forces of evil, suddenly appears on the horizon in the person of Jesus like a beautiful sunrise for all humanity to see! Many today believe Jesus offers personal escape from the chaos of our world with a one-way trip to heaven when we die. No doubt He provides millions of people with something to live for in our broken world. But I believe it's more than that. I believe that He actually gives us something worth dying for, not just something worth believing! The mission to which we have been called becomes clear when you take a deeper look at what motivated Jesus.

Follow The Clues

If you think back in our study on the times when the intensity of Jesus' heart was exposed, I think you will see an unmistakable pattern. Once you discover who and what triggered His anger, what made Him weep, and what made Him joyful and gave Him pleasure, you will sense the passions that made

Jesus who He was. We hear of Jesus' hopes and dreams for His followers. We see the intense feelings He experienced including profound grief, sadness, pain, and anger. These are valuable clues to the complex motivations of Jesus, not just examples of obedience and teachings for us to follow. We miss out if we only focus on what Jesus did or taught and fail to notice how he reacted. These motivations are a critical part of what we must learn from Jesus. It will always be a struggle. My motivations are not always pure. But I have found that His passions are contagious and clear for those who want to see them! And they all revolve around one central theme: restoration. He had a passion to restore personal freedom and dignity, a passion to restore our human value, and a passion to restore Truth and unity to humanity. Following Jesus, truly embracing Him, means I allow these specific passions to infiltrate my heart.

Following the clues makes love uncomfortably specific. I have to give up my human idea of love. I have to set aside vague intentions and feelings of warmth for others for something practical and costly. To see the clues, I have to want the treasure (Matthew 13:44)! I believe this is why Jesus exposed His heart—so we could see the treasure hidden in Him. Let me share a bit more about His three contagious passions, these treasures hidden in the life of Jesus.

A Passion To Restore Personal Freedom And Dignity

I think it is odd that we never hear of Jesus being angry at politicians, Rome, the bad economy, bad healthcare, bad public services, or bad people. He never rages against "the man," social injustices, or the political system. We see plenty of passion about these things among Christians today. But Jesus seemed more passionate about the loss of human dignity and enslavement to self than He did about rotten conditions. He spoke out against the destructive things that control our hearts—things like doubt, fear, greed, worry, self-centeredness, envy, hate, or material goods. But He was equally concerned about *who* controls our hearts (religious leaders, family, friends, or even Satan).

Jesus was angered by His own Jewish culture's religious practices. It did not sit well with Him when He saw corrupt religious leaders using oppression to build a kingdom for themselves. He accused them of being liars and murderers! Jesus twice disrupted the temple market, angrily calling out the merchants as a den of thieves and literally overturning their system. He saw how merchants worked in cahoots with religious leaders to pay for rebuilding "their" temple at the expense of God's honor. We see Him angrily confronting religious leaders who had usurped God's authority for their own purposes. Jesus intentionally antagonized them by performing miracles on the Sabbath. I think it was His way of saying that the Creator, who had established the Sabbath, never rested from doing good. The only concern of the Pharisees was using the law to maintain their status.

Unlike the religious leaders, Jesus was passionate about freeing the oppressed and honoring the weak. He was the Good Shepherd. We see Him freely offering His Kingdom to the sick, the sinner, the meek, the poor, and the blind. As far as Jesus was concerned, the "least of these" became the greatest when they simply gave what they had received from Him. Just a cup of water would do! He would seek the lost and guard those in His flock.

How did Jesus live in a world of political and religious oppression where the very lives He came to restore were unloved and grossly devalued? Jesus' strategy was to expose the lies and corruption and to love His enemies rather than bow to the same hunger for power they exhibited. He did not play Satan's game (remember the temptations in the wilderness?). Jesus was more concerned about the destruction of the soul than the destruction of the body. He respected authority, and He simply called everyone who would listen into the freedom of His new Kingdom. He challenged His followers to live with dignity as a holy nation, as a new people who loved God and loved their oppressors, as new branches on the Vine in God's vineyard! It was the heart of Jesus for the oppressed that drove Him to this extreme approach to His mission. It was His greatest joy to restore dignity and declare the captives free!

A Passion To Restore Human Value

Jesus' anger was triggered when He saw people using social standing and cultural traditions to breed prejudice and injustice. He lived in a world where love had grown cold, and self-preservation was the goal. Human life was cheapened by political and religious oppression and slavery. Occupation by Rome was bad enough, but those who wanted to impose cultural Jewish

178

traditions on everyone (like ceremonial handwashing) were intolerable to Jesus. They missed the irony of their attempt to make the nation "pure" by religious oppression. In reality, the whole nation was defiled by soiled hearts, not soiled hands.

The heart of Jesus for the disempowered was obvious. He enjoyed seeing the outcasts of society walking with Him, the Creator of the universe! He chose young fishermen, merchants, and a tax collector to be His disciples, not the religious elite. He placed children (who had no social standing) at His side, literally in the center of His circle, and suggested His disciples go drown themselves if they didn't like it! Jesus angrily rejected the prejudice against the Samaritans (a renegade Jewish tribe), women (in a patriarchal society), Gentiles (idolaters), tax collectors (traitors to Israel), Romans (the oppressors), prostitutes (sinners), and lepers (unclean). In fact, He enjoyed time with them! Jesus passionately believed in the spirit of the law of God, which was designed to express divine love and restore value to human life.

I am reminded of Jesus' poignant dialogue with Peter. Just before His ascension to the throne, Jesus lovingly and graciously asks him to feed His sheep. Despite Peter's disloyalty in the palace courtyard, Jesus trusts him to follow His example as a good shepherd, to be a source of love and life for others. Peter is empowered by Jesus' simple words. His value is restored, and he goes on to become the leader of the movement that changes the world. (In the end, Peter gave his life for the mission just like Jesus did, though tradition has it that he insisted on being crucified upside down.)

I can't help but see Jesus smile as Peter later writes a letter encouraging others to see their value to the King of Kings as a royal priesthood, a holy nation, chosen by God as member as the human race to proclaim His excellence to the world (1 Peter 2:9-10).

A Passion For Truth And Unity

One final passion we see in the Life of Jesus is particularly hard for us to understand in our culture. We must deal with the fact that Jesus' anger was triggered by rebellion against Truth. He was grieved by the disloyalty of Israel to the Truth about God. This rebellion had resulted in their downfall. It is why the Jewish people were divided and then scattered among the nations instead of being a light to the world. He hated their tolerance of injustice and their lack of righteousness. The failure of His own people, Israel, made this passion personal for Jesus!

Jesus was not all sweetness and light in His mission. Jesus lived in a world of faithlessness, unrighteousness, and disunity. Yes, He was the Light of the World, but this meant His life and teachings exposed lies and unrighteousness. During His years of teaching, He wielded a sword of Truth and divided families. But He also unashamedly offered friendship to those who kept His commandments. In His parables, He promised peace and unity but only to those who had ears to hear. There were wheat and tares, sheep and goats. Not everyone entered His new Kingdom. The Way was narrow—defined by the Truth about His Father.

It was Jesus' passion to restore peace and build a new community among the disenfranchised and the lonely. He wanted to save His people from the sin that was destroying them. Like a Good Shepherd, Jesus was providing a path for the flock to safe pastures. Like a Vine, He was the point of connection for all who wanted Life. Like He and His Father, He prays we can all be one in the Truth. One flock, one Shepherd, one Vine, one Kingdom. Jesus uses His Father's Word to call people to repentance. His Voice became the single point of focus for all who would be restored. It was out of His passion for Truth and unity that Jesus invited all people into a new spiritual Kingdom. But the choice to accept the Truth was theirs.

Mission Accomplished!

It all comes down to this: You can't fully experience the importance of being human without acting on the importance of embracing Jesus. And, you cannot act on the importance of embracing Jesus without first acknowledging the importance of being human. It all works together! My books *Finding the Way, The Importance of Being Human,* and *The Importance of Embracing Jesus* are intended to paint this picture. I truly hope I have succeeded to some degree.

I would encourage you to use the list of feature stories and the headlines in this book to keep you inspired and oriented about the realities of the spiritual realm. Our world, and certainly our Western culture, is focused on taking from us, and it gives very little in return. But in the realm of Jesus we receive what we need to live as human beings created in the image of God.

What a privilege. What a gift. In the end, we are glorified with Him when He is glorified in us! Make no mistake about it—His glory is above us all! I have no doubt He accomplished His mission to establish His Kingdom. To this day, you can find evidence of it in a remnant of loyal followers whose lives say it all. To them I say, "Mission forward!" To the rest I say, "Join the team!" We are all part of His incredible mission.

It's All In The Eyes

A final note to all those who, like me, sometimes just want to hear the bottom line. I hope you are convinced that embracing Jesus is of utmost importance. But if it is, how do we do it? After all, Jesus isn't here for us to literally embrace. Is it more about embracing the idea of Jesus? Or maybe just embracing the things He taught as worthwhile ideals for life? If Jesus is alive (as I believe He is), then to me it must be more than that. But what? And how does that work?

To answer this question, some emphasize the importance of the words of the Bible, some the presence of His Spirit. Some emphasize the presence of God within, some the presence of God in community and in our world. All good answers . . . but not totally satisfying. I brought up this question to a group of guys as I was finishing this book as a sort of reality check. I wasn't sure I had really answered the question. A friend suggested it may be as simple as seeing Jesus in others. He reminded me that we use our eyes to connect with our world and with each other. He pointed out that even our pets know this: they will look us in the eye when it's time for their treat or look away when they don't want to listen to our command. Of course, I was thrilled since, as an ophthalmologist, I can at last point out the importance of the eyes!

I was reminded that the eyes are indeed the window to the soul. We look into the eyes of others to communicate, to connect, to share ourselves. Jesus restored sight as both a gift to the physically blind and as an illustration of His spiritual mission. Jesus looked in His disciples' eyes and often saw doubt and fear, but He also saw hope and courage. Dare I say, I think He could see Himself living in them and, one day, through them! He knew they sometimes looked away but encouraged them to abide in Him—to keep their eyes on Him. And once Jesus left physically, they would need to see Him in each other. They would need to love each other as He had loved them!

I am convinced that the Word of God speaks to us today and that the Holy Spirit connects us to the heart of God and His power. I know that the Kingdom of God is within those who have put their faith in Jesus and that it is expressed in the community (body) of Christ in our world. But maybe we are designed to embrace these great truths with our senses, especially our eyes. Mother Theresa saw Jesus in the poor of Calcutta. Maybe we should look for Jesus in the faces of our family, friends, and neighbors, and in the guy who serves us at a restaurant and the lady who checks us out at the store. In some eyes there is only darkness. Many look away. But in others, no matter how dim, there is light. Even those who are physically blind can somehow sense it. I am not suggesting we embrace everyone in some "Kumbaya" lifestyle (as one friend put it so well!). I am suggesting that embracing Jesus is ultimately experienced by a life of expectancy, a life of seeing Jesus wherever He is. *Heavenly Father, give us eyes to see your Beloved Son working in our world and in the lives of others!*

Appendix 1.

How to start a conversation that grows a community of faith

Why Are Questions So Important?

We are not very good at listening to each other. We are more interested in asserting our opinions or telling our stories than taking time to hear someone else's. Our bandwidth for genuine engagement is quite limited. It's hard to even convince someone that you do actually want to listen. It's almost as if you need some sort of "I'm listening" signal. I have found that sincere questions can be helpful tools for engaging with others.

Questions help us fill the many gaps in our understanding. We ask simple *who, what, where, when,* and *why* questions to clarify, expand, and prioritize the information we need to make good decisions about ourselves and our relationships. We ask *how* things work to help us process the complexity of our world and overcome our limitations. We ask *what if, why not, why here,* and *why now* questions to explore and create.

The funny thing is, questions are not just tools. They also tell us a lot about ourselves. When you ask someone to explain something, it's usually because *you* have a specific interest. What you want to know reveals a bit of who you are, and by asking, you are helping the speaker know how to best engage with you to keep the conversation going. In this way, thoughtful, respectful questions can provide the stimulus for the development of trust and mutual respect. I would go so far as to say that sincere questions are at the heart of growing relationships. No doubt, trust and respect are critical. But relationships won't grow unless you engage in meaningful dialogue. You can't walk together unless you can talk together!

I think it makes sense to get more intentional about asking questions to build relationships. Many of our day-to-day conversations are casual and shallow, even impersonal. There's nothing wrong with that unless that's all you ever do. We, as followers of Jesus, need to ask questions that go a little deeper. Most people feel a bit awkward asking too many questions—it makes you feel like you're intruding in someone else's business. I agree. Good questions are not about satisfying our personal curiosity or getting the latest gossip. I have found that the trick to relationship-building questions is learning to ask questions that *others* feel are worth answering.

Asking Questions That Matter

If you want to grow a relationship, you must learn how to ask questions that matter at a relational level. It seems like it should be pretty easy. In practice, it's not. We normally raise questions only when we need information and avoid any serious questions when we are trying to relate to others. "How's it goin'?" "What do you do?" and "Where do you live?" questions are good enough openers. But it's hard to go beyond the awkward silence that usually follows.

Let me give you some specific guidelines that have helped me ask questions that matter to others. To know what, when, and how to ask good relational questions:

1. Listen for how others see themselves, not just what they do.
2. Listen for what others value, not just what they have.
3. Find the right time and place for asking questions to clarify and go deeper.
4. Let your face and your words communicate respect and consideration for the feelings and experiences of others.
5. Be ready to honestly answer questions about yourself.

It may be as easy as dropping a simple question into a casual conversation that lets someone know you are really listening. For example, as you listen to someone talk about their recent vacation, ask what they valued the most about their time away. They may reply with an example of something they enjoyed, but remind them that you are asking them to share what they *valued*. Remember that you are not the judge of their values—they are! Or as another example, it may be that you sense the emotional pain of someone you bump into at the supermarket. A simple, sincere question about how their day is going may reveal a real need. If they make eye contact and you are willing to initiate it, offer a brief prayer and a little encouragement for them right there in the store!

It doesn't take much to ask effective questions that create opportunities for deeper relationships. Then you have only to decide what you are going to do with these opportunities.

How To Get A Discussion Group Going

We all have agendas when we meet with others. It may be for simple enjoyment or for achieving certain tasks. Sometimes we meet with others to solve problems; sometimes for personal support and growth; or sometimes we get together just for a sense of belonging. These are all good reasons to meet with others.

Unfortunately, we rarely get together to discuss things that matter. A good discussion group can make a huge difference in your perspective over a period of time. As a follower of Jesus, I think they are essential. Jesus can and does speak through others! I am not the only one with the mind of Christ—ALL who have faith in Him are a new creation with a new Voice in their hearts (1 Corinthians 2:16, Galatians 2:20). Why should I miss out on that?

Groups of five to six people are ideal for having discussions. This is large enough to ensure some diversity but small enough to make sure everyone is heard. My wife and I have hosted dozens of home groups over many years and each group is unique. There is no cookie-cutter formula for what will work. Sometimes we offer a light meal, sometimes not. Sometimes we discuss topics, sometimes we discuss the Bible. Our groups have included music teams, international surgical eye teams, friends, family, Muslims, agnostics, churchgoers, and non-churchgoers.

There are some common denominators in the groups that have worked the best. First and foremost, effective discussion groups are relational. They revolve around questions that matter in real life, not facts you can find in a textbook or online chats. The discussions are not esoteric, but they are deep. Second, our best discussion groups are aspirational. They share a joy in discovery and in solving problems. They really believe that God is challenging us to greater things and are not afraid to take some risks to find what God wants them to do. Last but not least, the most effective discussion groups are inspirational. They believe that God is speaking through His Word and each other. They ask questions that Jesus might want to answer. They encourage and support each other. There is a sense that God has been part of the discussion.

Most often, our discussion groups started as a simple conversation with someone. And the conversations started by asking a few questions that mattered to them. Everything from a meeting with a group of guys from our neighborhood around the firepit, to a neighborhood Bible study, to a church home group can be traced back to this beginning. Remember, if we get intentional about *why* we are meeting together with others, it guides *how* we do it.

Here are some simple rules about how to do small group discussions:

1. Come with something to share. Very simple ideas can have profound meaning.
2. Come ready to learn from others. Expect Jesus to show up in others who know Him.
3. Come expecting to do a little work to discover something new. It may take a little digging to get the richest treasure.
4. Come to be constructive, not complaining. Take time for someone who is struggling but suggest one-on-one time to delve into it.

Not all groups will be a good fit for you. Don't worry if you feel you need to move on if it's just not working. But remember, in so far as it is up to you, if you act like a member of the group, you can generally be a member of the group.

We love it when we see the group interacting together as a whole, in huddles, and one-on-one. We are encouraged when we see participants asking each other questions that really matter and sharing thoughts that make the experience meaningful and fun for everyone. Real dialogue is occurring and, as a result, significant growth. Healthy groups may appear to be messy and unpredictable, but they are usually joyful. There is a sense of dignity and mutual respect. People in healthy groups embrace each other across cultural and social lines. They model virtuous and sacrificial living.

Sometimes we need questions that stir the imagination and dialogue that broadens our perspective. Sometimes we just need encouragement and relaxation. But we always need questions that grow our relationships with one another and with Jesus!

The Importance Of Community

The challenge of doing a study like this is not intellectual, it's cultural. We like the convenience of personal Bible study and just listening to Bible teaching on our own. Self-study and "me time" are the norm for personal growth. We don't have time for the messiness and uncertainty of group discussions. This cultural problem starts with a firm belief in individualism—*my* story is what matters. We look inward for Truth rather than listening to others. As a result, we tend to create bubbles around ourselves using wealth and technology. We demand personal space. We build churches that tell us what we want to hear and surround ourselves with people just like us.

We think we need a castle to protect our stuff rather than a community or neighborhood in which we share and grow. The American dream is having a home (or at least my own space), not a community. We know how to find a good house with a solid foundation, structural integrity, and all the features we want. But we don't know what we should be looking for in people. We're better at finding good houses than we are at finding a healthy community or healthy relationships.

Let me just say up front that while there is no such thing as a perfect community, there *is* such a thing as a *healthy* community. Signs of good health usually include diversity of age and background, a shared vision for life and well-being, a pattern of open communication, respect for personal space, shared responsibility, and shared authority. These are the things that define the solid foundation, structural integrity, and a safe, comfortable environment of a beneficial community. (Check out Chapter 15 in my book *The Importance of Being Human* for more information about how you are designed as a human being to experience community.)

I would bet that not many readers have ever experienced a healthy community. But there is a good chance that, over time, the group of people who have joined you in your investigation of the incredible story of Jesus will become exactly that. Healthy communication and shared stories tend to produce healthy communities! It might be just what you need once you finish with this guide: a small group of people around you, sharing life together, held together by a common vision for something more than what our culture seems to offer.

Keep The Dialogue Going

How do you keep the dialogue going? By the time you finish *The Importance of Embracing Jesus,* you will likely have more questions—good questions. This guide immerses you in a Story that can engage you for a lifetime and gives you the tools you need to explore it! I would suggest you continue to ask, "What's the story here?" as you consider the life and teachings of Jesus. Keep leaning into the importance of being human and continue taking time for reflection and time with God. There are literally hundreds of good questions that need discussion. I encourage you to keep looking for the story behind the facts and the meaning behind the Truth. Challenge each other and, by doing so, learn to love each other. And in all of it, keep your eyes open for Jesus to show up! You know that He will!

Appendix 2:

A practical approach to spending time with God

By Steve Arrowsmith

My friend Glenn Strauss has worked tirelessly with me on improving my communication with my wife. Frequently, I am sure I have said things just the right way, yet my wife fails to react in the way I think my well-thought-out pearls of wisdom should accomplish. At his most eloquent, Glenn's gentle guidance for me has been to "JUST SHUT UP!" And he is right. Often, I need to just let my wife talk, even if (or maybe *especially* if) I don't get what she is saying; in these times, I just need to "be" for her, rather than to "say" to her.

How do we "just be" in the presence of God? How do we listen to a Voice, which needs no words to communicate? God bends very low to speak and listen to us. This seems to be one of the huge examples of His grace. Think about the mind-blowing immensity of God, and then imagine how it could possibly work for a micro-worm like me to communicate with Him. Glenn's "JUST SHUT UP" approach, known by several other names in spiritual circles, is one way, not the only way, to communicate with God. We recognize the yawning gap between His greatness and our limitations. In that immense presence, we just be quiet. This is a tool to open an alternate pathway by which God can communicate directly with our inner being. Rather than trying vainly to be eloquent, humble, contrite, powerful, smart, or Biblical in my attempts to dialogue with Him, this practice leaves it all to God. Speaking to us directly, He expands our souls.

The practice really refuses to fit into any of our "modern" spiritual language. "Meditation?" Not quite. No "Oms" or incense required. "Centered prayer" doesn't really totally embrace the concept for me, either. If your "center" is a place of inner peace and absolute quiet, good enough. "Contemplative prayer" may be the most common term out there, though some might find the sound of the term a bit spooky. The gist is just listening and not talking. All of this dates to the very beginnings of God's interaction with human beings. For centuries, since the birth of the Church, Christians have quietly invited God to interact directly with our souls. From this rich history, we find there is a process to guide Christians to enjoy this discipline. This is one of those vexing things in life that is, at the same time, both simple and difficult. Maybe it was easier for 3rd century Church Fathers to be silent than it is for us in our era of over-stimulation. You no doubt will discover, as I have, how hard it is to get one's brain to quiet down. There are many good books and articles on how to get started with this practice. As a place to start, you might try this website, which briefly summarizes the basic steps:

https://guidedchristianmeditation.com/2515/meditation/what-is-contemplative-prayer-and-how-to-do-a-contemplative-prayer-practice/

Early in the process of learning to do this, I found the main skill I needed was self-forgiveness. Many times, I find myself thinking about some silly email I got earlier that day or some favorite Eagles' tune from 1977. And all I can do is internally laugh and go on. Expect learning the discipline of quieting down spiritually to be a process, not an event.

The other "hard" part for me is overcoming my expectation to have some immediate and tangible change or benefit. I open my eyes, sure that I will have some new insight or revelation. But this is not how it works. The communication that goes on is in an area of the soul one might label as our unconscious. I was taught to expect that I would gradually and subtly feel more in tune with God, more loving, patient, more at peace, and more whole. My initial reaction was, "What bunk that is!" In all my discussions with those who practice this discipline, I never heard anyone really describe how this works or feels. I remember asking my pastor about it. After he explained that his main challenge (as he did this early every morning) was to stay awake, he finally replied, "I have absolutely no idea." Ha! I thought, *Got him!* Then I asked if he thought it had really done anything for him. "I can't think of any other spiritual practice that has changed me more" was the answer. Now I must admit that the same has proven to be true for me. Something unexplainable and wonderful bubbles up from deep inside. And it is real!

So, as you think about the potentially life-altering insights in this book and want to build them into your own heart and life, I can't think of a better way to accomplish this than by learning and practicing a *heart open to listening* to instead of talking to God. This book is not meant or able to be a treatise on any specific method, but we hope it inspires you to learn more, do the initially challenging work, and in a fresh, deep, and everlasting way, "Embrace Jesus." Our part is to invite Him in, then listen to Glenn's advice, and just shut up. Full stop.

Acknowledgments

Thanks to all who have contributed to the writing and development of this book. Thanks to the Saturday morning "council of faith" guys and my home group who have listened to my questions for a couple of years now and still seem to be interested! So many insights have come from each of you. Special thanks to Mark Bergman for your suggestion that it's all in the eyes and Buddy Sloan for keeping us from getting too sappy about it all!

So many others have helped get me over the finish line in writing this last book in the series. Thanks especially to Jerry Christensen and Steve Morris, two guys God put right in my neighborhood to encourage, provide input, and help build a vision for how God could use this work. Thanks to my dear friend Art Hill who offered many suggestions and corrections but mostly for his affirming friendship. And to Brian and Pauline Harris and Randy Randall for their support and encouragement. I could not have done it without all the discussions we had!

Thanks to my son Jonathan for his contributions and encouragement. It means a lot to me! Thanks to Karen Steinmann for her editorial work and many great suggestions and to Roaring Lambs for their encouragement and assistance in publication. Thanks to Steve Arrowsmith for his vital contribution to the book regarding contemplative prayer. You da man!

Thanks to my sweetheart for her patience and encouragement. I promise I am done writing! Now let's enjoy some camping!

www.ingramcontent.com/pod-product-compliance
Lightning Source LLC
Chambersburg PA
CBHW081328090426
42737CB00017B/3058